RODEO

RODEO

Behind the Scenes at America's Most Exciting Sport

Lynn Campion

The Lyons Press
Guilford, Connecticut
An Imprint of The Globe Pequot Press

COVER PHOTO: Scott Johnston rides I'm No Copenhagen Angel, a well-known bronc owned by Cotton Rosser. The Australian lives in Gustine, Texas, where he is much closer to the high-paying North American rodeo circuit. Scott is one of very few cowboys to be ranked among the top fifteen in the world in two events: bareback and saddle bronc riding.

PREVIOUS PAGE: Stock contractor Ike Sankey gives a wide berth to one of his bulls as he rounds up his stock for a trip to the Cody Night Rodeo.

The Lyons Press is an imprint of The Globe Pequot Press.

Text Design: M.A. Dube

Library of Congress Cataloging-in-Publication Data
Campion, Lynn.
    Rodeo : behind the scenes at America's most exciting sport / Lynn Campion.
        p. cm.
Includes index.
    ISBN 1-59228-405-1 (Paper)
    ISBN 1-58574-665-7 (Case)
    1. Rodeos—United States. 2. Rodeo performers—United States. I. Title: Behind the scenes at America's most exciting sport. II. Title.
    GV1834.5 .C36 2002
    791.84—dc21   2002011296

Printed in CANADA

10 9 8 7 6 5 4 3 2

To my parents,
my family,
and to my husband, Ted.

Contents

Foreword

AS A YOUNG BOY GROWING UP ON A FARM WEST OF LITTLETON, COLORADO, I was excited to go to the National Western Rodeo in Denver with my dad. I remember Cy Taillon, the announcer, and his gravelly voice. I remember meeting the clown Wilbur Plaugher, and also General Manager Willard Simms, who sat me in his box next to the timer. Wow!

My youthful excitement evolved into a later understanding of, and a deep appreciation for, this great American sport. For the past 25 years, I have enjoyed working with Chuck Sylvester, General Manager of the National Western, who is truly dedicated to rodeo.

Rodeo surely captures the essence of great sport: dramatic action, the adrenaline rush of exciting entertainment, and the tough, rugged, and incalculable ability and competitiveness of its star contestants—the cowboy and cowgirl. Matching their ability and grit with the raw power and strength of roughstock is the essential contest that draws and attracts so many youth and adults alike. The horsemanship and talent of rider and mount in the timed events are a wonder to behold.

But rodeo is much more than mere competition: it is an expression of our western heritage that provides a unique perspective on our history. Trailing cattle to the trailhead; providing beef as a critical food staple for the burgeoning population back East; and ranchers raising cattle on our grassy plains—all conjure up romantic notions of the range cowboy today.

Life for the cowboy was rough, and it embraced the rugged challenges of simple survival. Endless hours on horseback in all manner of weather helped nurture the values that we aspire to today: independence, self-assurance, dependability, courage, and fortitude in the face of great obstacles. And so we are able to learn from rodeo as well. It becomes a metaphor of life for us all to cherish.

This book—a real treasure by Lynn Campion—brings us close to the people of rodeo, their passion, and their profession. You will "see" behind the scenes; you will catch glimpses of the many individuals and the parts they play in producing rodeo— a real extravaganza.

Also, let us not forget—indeed, let us express our gratitude, to the rodeo sponsors—Coors, Wrangler, Dodge Trucks, U.S. Smokeless Tobacco, and many others—for their crucial support!

Patrick A. Grant, President
The Western Stock Show Association
July 3, 2002

A YOUNG BUCKAROO, WITH DAD BY HIS SIDE, IS READY TO TACKLE THE
COMPETITION IN MUTTON BUSTIN', A SPECIAL EVENT ADDED TO SOME
OF THE SUMMER RODEOS, IN WHICH CHILDREN RIDE SHEEP.

RAIN OR SHINE, THE ROUGHSTOCK COWBOYS GATHER IN AN AREA BEHIND THE CHUTES WHERE THEY ARE ALLOWED SOME PRIVACY WHILE THEY PREPARE. A TRADITIONAL PART OF RODEO, THIS RITUAL IS SLOWLY GIVING WAY TO INDOOR ARENAS, GUARDS, AND CONCRETE DRESSING ROOMS.

Author's Note and Acknowledgments

RODEO HAS ALWAYS been a part of my life. The sport has seen many changes since it was formalized, especially during the last two decades. While I was photographing at a Fourth of July rodeo in Montana several years ago, the differences became more apparent to me. Not only was the livestock of a higher caliber than the animals I'd seen in my youth, but the local favorites were being challenged by a new group of competitors: out-of-state pros. I became curious about the changes—and so began my examination of modern rodeo and how best to present it. This was a challenge. On one hand, the settling of the West has been idealized and made into something it wasn't. I didn't want to contribute further to myth or glamorize the rodeo cowboy. On the other hand, this sport deserves to be better understood and celebrated. Modern rodeo is a competition of highly skilled professionals, most of whom have emerged from a shared way of life, one that they will most likely return to when their competitive days are over. These cowboys pursue excellence in the same manner as other pro athletes, yet they receive very little outside financial support, must pay their own travel expenses and entry fees, and come away empty-handed unless they win.

There are many people who helped me understand more about today's rodeo stock, what is involved in each event, and what a contestant has to do to win:

- ✻ Kelly Wardell is the first person I'd like to recognize and thank. His quiet focus and deep knowledge of horses, rodeo, and spur-making helped launch my decision to write about the sport. His girlfriend, Barb Patterson, filled in some spaces and added her enthusiasm for the project. The two introduced me around, and I went on from there.

- ✻ Marvin Garrett also helped me early on. He gave me a good deal of insight into the complexities of bareback riding while teaching a three-day clinic at the College of Southern Idaho. Marvin was still healing from a broken back that he suffered in a tragic plane accident involving several cowboys, but he is now fully recovered, winning again—and still helping others learn.

- ✻ Ike and Roberta Sankey allowed me to accompany them on long rides to round up their stock, and helped me go behind the scenes at many rodeos around the country. Both have tremendous knowledge and deep respect for the sport. Roberta also helped by reading over part of the manuscript and clarifying technicalities. As for Ike—well, he's a pro who works extremely hard to ensure the success of his stock.

- ✻ John Growney is probably still shaking his head at my sudden appearances in Red Bluff and my many questions, but he nonetheless trusted in my intentions, and I am grateful.

- ✻ Dennis Tryan took a lot of time to help me understand all aspects of roping. Not only does he train some great horses and help many riders hone their skills, he is also the father of two young men who are going for broke in team roping.

- ✻ Will Rasmussen made himself available by phone whenever I needed further explanation about something.

- ✻ Billy Etbauer doesn't even know what a beacon he has been to others—including me. I've watched him prepare, ride, win, lose, and help fellow competitors. His style and incredible focus are qualities we all would like to emulate.

- ✻ To Deb Greenough, Rod Lyman, Kristie Peterson: a very special thanks to each of you for allowing me into your lives.

✳ I had editorial help from several different sources. Of course, my editor, Enrica Gadler, is the first to thank. She worked on this book from the get-go. Another editor and friend, Kirk Robertson, did his utmost to help me when I thought this whole thing wasn't going to survive. Kirk, you got me started again. Thank you.

✳ My grown-up children were integral to this project because they believed in me. They also know how to write and edit. Thank you, Berit and Ashley.

✳ And the biggest note of thanks goes to my husband, Theodore Waddell: amazing artist, rancher, friend, and mentor. Ted gave me the courage to explore and record what I saw as something unique and special—which it is.

Introduction

HEN I WAS A LITTLE GIRL GROWING up in Denver, one of the most exciting things to see was the National Western Stock Show. My parents would take me and my brother to the livestock barn where the animals were being groomed and fussed over. Then we would watch the judging, where every cow looked her shiny best. We got to see teams of draft horses standing knee deep in straw while they were rigged with polished harnesses and brass bells. I remember watching all of the broncs and bulls while they were being sorted and then moved, single file, through a maze of chutes. We were especially fascinated by the cowboys. These guys were either whirling their ropes in the air, stretching their legs, working on their gear, or riding around on beautiful horses. Of course, the RODEO itself was the culmination of every visit—icing on the cake. My parents must have shown me a good deal about this entire tradition and sport, because it still tugs at me. Rodeo is a big part of our heritage and should be celebrated as such.

Later on, I competed at the National Western, although in a very different category than my Western counterparts: the Horse Show. To the rodeo cowboys, a teenage girl wandering around long rows of stalls dressed in jodhpurs and shiny black boots was probably something to behold. Regardless, I did learn how to manage the pressure of showing my horse in front of a big crowd—a prelude to some great years of cutting horse competition. But the rodeo cowboys always held my interest. Not only were they from a background I was quite familiar with, they were tough, polite, focused, and more introspective than competitors from the English side of the barn. I switched to Western and never looked back.

As a young woman, I married and moved to Idaho and then to Montana, where we raised a family and ran cattle on our ranch near Darby. We always found good horses to work the cattle, and I've been lucky to have had some great ones—especially my Woody, who is still alive and always close by.

WORLD CHAMPION DEB GREENOUGH WARMS UP WHILE QUIETLY SURVEYING FAMILIAR RODEO GROUNDS. ALTHOUGH HIS BRONC FELL ON HIM AFTER IT LEFT THE CHUTE, DEB CONTINUED RODEOING UNTIL MID-SUMMER, WHEN HIS INJURIES TOOK THEIR TOLL. HE THEN MADE THE DECISION TO RETIRE, BUT WAITED UNTIL HE WAS HEALED UP AND COULD FINISH HIS STELLAR CAREER IN STYLE—WHICH HE DID, ON HOME TURF, RIDING A MONTANA BRONC THAT HAD BEEN RAISED BY HIS COLLEGE RODEO COACH, STOCK CONTRACTOR IKE SANKEY.

Together, Woody and I won many national cutting futurities. His great spirit and willingness to learn and work hard led me to write my first book, *Training and Showing the Cutting Horse.*

A professional photographer for over thirty years now, I've always focused on people and the process they go through to excel. Whether it be ski racing, teaching, creating art, or anything in between, if someone truly loves what he's doing and is absorbed in the process, I'll want to photograph and write about him. This interest has threaded its way back to rodeo and the life surrounding what remains of our West. For the past six years, I've been photographing rodeo athletes, learning their stories, and observing their passion for what they do. Today's rodeo cowboys are a fascinating modern generation that is rooted in the land and its traditions. They represent the best that we were and what we honor. As they try to raise their skills to the highest level, these men and women are consummate professionals, and are totally dedicated. But even among fans, little is known about what they go through while striving to reach the top, or what happens during competition when the crowd is cheering and the pressure is on.

FUTURE CHAMPIONS GATHER BEHIND THE CHUTES TO DISCUSS THE WORLD'S PROBLEMS WHILE THEY GET READY FOR THE MUTTON BUSTIN' EVENT.

Very few rodeo cowboys are out there touting their profession or are motivated solely by the desire for fame, even though prize money, television coverage, and sponsorship have increased dramatically in the past decade. They aren't the type—which was my initial impression as a child—and most of them couldn't even sneak up on vanity or inflated egos. Theirs is a quiet but fierce camaraderie, unusual in our world today. They spend a lifetime pursuing a dream that percolates through the early years of ranch life or through other experiences involving animals. I hope this book adds some understanding to what these athletes have to do to get where they are. At the very least, I hope it enhances your next visit to one of our many rodeos.

A Brief History of Rodeo

"RODEOS," OR ROUNDUPS (FROM THE SPANISH word *rodear*, meaning "to surround"), have been present in North America since the Spanish first brought horses and cattle to the Southwest in the 1500s. As cattle herds grew larger, cowboys (known in Spanish as *vaqueros*) on horseback were needed to manage them. The word rodeo took on added meaning with the advent of the gold rush and the ensuing demand for food in the mid-1800s. Well-known trails were formed by the great cattle drives, pointing north from Texas through New Mexico and Arizona to the open summer ranges of Colorado, Wyoming, and Montana. Cow camps and ranches sprang up along the way, vaqueros became known in English as buckaroos, and then as cowboys—and rodeo referred to the small competitions cow hands held during their roundups. In Montana Territory, for example, a typical spring roundup covered over 400 miles of open prairie. Cowboys from different ranches would get together to separate, brand, and doctor the animals.

In the early days when time was not afforded a cowboy to fully train every animal, wild horses were rounded up, roped, and held down until a saddle was strapped on and a skilled rider could climb aboard. "Green broke" horses were all a cow hand needed to help him tend cattle. Work was certainly easier, and pay was definitely better, for those who could ride well and handle a rope. Some riders had a knack for staying in the saddle no matter how hard a bronc bucked. Others could rope and immobilize a steer with lightning speed and accuracy. These were the ones others watched from the corral fences. Their reputations grew, and when the big spring roundups occurred, contests naturally followed.

As land in the West became more desirable and trains and fences forced the cattle industry to localize, Wild West shows were largely responsible for keeping the rodeo tradition alive. Entertainment was slowly replacing necessity, even though working cattle from horseback continued to be normal ranch procedure. Today, the term rodeo has come to mean a contest of professional or semi-professional athletes—most with a background in ranch life—competing for thousands of dollars in prize money at organized events. In fact, rodeo is the only sport we have that grew out of an occupation and way of life.

Although rodeo historians differ as to whether the very first true spectator rodeo in our country was held in New Mexico, Colorado, or Texas, other states followed suit during the late

1800s. Roundups, fiestas, or stampedes were recorded as having also taken place in Arizona, Kansas, Wyoming, Montana, and western Canada. In stockyards, corrals, or in an area without fences, these contests cropped up more and more often. Admission was charged at a Denver rodeo, prize money was awarded at one in Pecos, and a fully organized "Cowboy Tournament" occurred in Prescott. The sport, aided greatly by "Buffalo Bill" Cody's Wild West show, became an added bonus to Fourth of July celebrations across the country. Competition

and entertainment enticed people to come to town and spend money with local merchants. There were planning committees who organized and produced the events, stockmen who provided the animals, and rules to abide by. There were grand entry parades with dignitaries and contestants riding pretty horses to bring in the steers, as well as trick riders, bronc busting, and fancy roping. There were also cowhands who came from all over to compete for prizes and a bit of money. And we still follow the same format. Indeed, to this day, the most valuable possession a cowboy or cowgirl owns is a championship belt buckle or saddle earned at a top rodeo.

As trains crossed more territory, and Wild West shows merged together with rodeos, more events evolved and bigger audiences came to performances such as Cheyenne Frontier Days, the Calgary Stampede, and the Pendleton Roundup. The new events of steer wrestling, bareback, and steer riding were added (bulls were not used before 1925 and did not fully replace steers until 1954), women often competed against men, and prize money grew. Then, in 1929, the Rodeo Association of America was organized by several of the rodeo producers. Their rules for conduct and competition helped to standardize the events, but the cowboys were often exploited by big promoters. In fact, after being coaxed east with promises of big prize money for shows at the Madison Square Garden and Boston Gardens, a group of cowboys had to band

WORLD CHAMPION HERBERT THERIOT'S SON, MARCUS, IS
A REGULAR ON THE RODEO CIRCUIT. HIS PREFERRED
SEATING IS ATOP EASY, WITH A ROPE IN HIS HANDS. EASY
WAS VOTED AMERICAN QUARTER HORSE ASSOCIATION'S
2001 CALF ROPING HORSE OF THE YEAR.

together to force the promoter to pay.
As a result, they formed the Cowboys'
Turtle Association in 1936, established
their own set of rules and regulations
for riders as well as animals, and
awarded year-end champions through
points earned and money won. In 1945,
the Turtles changed their name to the
Rodeo Cowboys Association. Their
actions set the stage for what has evolved
into today's largest organization of
cowboys: the Professional Rodeo
Cowboy's Association. Women formed
what is now called the Women's Pro
Rodeo Association, which sanctions the
barrel racing events at PRCA rodeos.
Their sister organization, the Professional Women's Rodeo Association,
holds a complete series of rodeos
specifically for women, in which they
can compete in bull riding and all the
other events traditionally reserved for
men.

Rodeo today is a lifestyle and a
passion for almost every one of these
athletes. They may have started out as
little kids who grew up around
animals or who traveled the circuit
with their parents. Or they might have
begun as teenagers who joined high
school or college rodeo clubs to learn

more about combining skills with riding. But when they were bitten by the rodeo bug and
decided to turn professional, they signed up for traveling American and Canadian highways
and airways, in all types of weather, for staying in nameless motels, and for a road-food diet
supplemented with bottomless cups of coffee.

ACTING AS A HAZER, ROD LYMAN HANGS BACK SLIGHTLY ON THIS HARD-RUNNING STEER SO HE
DOESN'T PUT MORE PRESSURE ON IT. IN DOING THIS, HE IS STILL ABLE TO TURN IT SLIGHTLY TOWARD
JUSTIN DAVIS, WHO MAKES A LONG, BUT SUCCESSFUL, REACH.

The sport has come a long way from the time when ranch hands tried to tame wild broncs
or doctor cattle within the confines of dusty, handmade enclosures. Now, rodeos are enjoyed
from fairground benches and arena seats by twenty million fans annually, and via satellite,
which brings ESPN International to 140 countries and 85 million households. Today's cowboys
and cowgirls have a chance to win over $200,000 in one year. But every rodeo contestant is still
an independent contractor who determines his or her own schedule, who pays to enter events
without any promise of money in return, and who can be on top one day and out for the year
the next. Our rodeo cowboy folk hero, though he can travel by jet and make calls from a cell
phone, still follows in the footsteps of those who came before him, carrying on a long tradition
with a deep respect for animals and livestock.

Preparations and Contract Personnel

An age-old tradition of
bringing in the steers
heralds the start of the
Red Bluff Roundup.

T HERE ARE VARIOUS types of rodeos, from junior, high school, and college rodeos to amateur and professional ones. Every rodeo follows rules that have been set by a governing organization. The oldest and largest organization in America is called the Professional Rodeo Cowboys Association. The PRCA requires contestants to be over the age of eighteen, pay membership dues, and comply with rules and bylaws in order to compete and earn prize money. The PRCA now has over eleven thousand members in the United States and Canada, a host of excellent sponsors, annually sanctions about seven hundred rodeos, and last year awarded prize money totaling over thirty million dollars. Although there are numerous other rodeo organizations, the PRCA rules and regulations are used as the standard in this book. Not only do they have a reciprocal agreement with the Canadian Professional Rodeo Association (CPRA) that allows Canadian competitors to qualify for championship events in the United States, but their high standards are widely accepted, and their policies are consistent with those of college and youth associations. Also, PRCA guidelines are dedicated to preserving the historical integrity of the entire sport of rodeo, ensuring dependable contract personnel, and strictly enforcing animal welfare regulations. A list of associations, professional and amateur, is included in the appendix.

JEFF SHEARER AND JULIO MORENO TURN THEIR SIGHTS TOWARD THE SADDLE BRONC AFTER MAKING SURE THE RIDER IS SAFE. WITH THE FLANK STRAP GONE, JULIO HAS A GOOD HOLD OF THE BRONC'S REIN SO HE CAN ESCORT IT SAFELY FROM THE ARENA.

Planning a sanctioned rodeo that will draw top contestants can take well over a year. First, a rodeo committee has to be formed and the numerous responsibilities delegated. Some members of a committee might be ranchers who have spent their lives around horses and cattle, and are familiar with the business. Many are former contestants who know the ins and outs of each event. Civic leaders are essential because they can help integrate rodeo into the fabric of their community, as well as secure financial backing. The rodeo committee must be able to comply with all PRCA regulations, adjust scheduling, and find sponsors and at least one good stock contractor to supply the livestock. Also, they must secure facilities that are adequate for every event and large enough to accommodate the anticipated number of contestants, animals, and spectators.

STRETCHING IS A NECESSARY COMPONENT OF EVERY ATHLETE'S PERFORMANCE.

Once the rodeo is approved and scheduled with a primary stock contractor, various personnel must be hired to make sure every aspect of the performance runs smoothly and professionally. From secretaries and announcers to those who provide cattle and bucking horses, these specialized men and women bring their expertise and love of the sport to every big rodeo across the country. Most have been involved in business and have had extensive experience around animals—invaluable to understanding and providing for a well-run show.

The rodeo office becomes a beehive of activity as the event draws near. Ordering feed and water for the stock, preparing the arena, providing contestants with information, dealing with traffic control, lighting, and wiring . . . these are just a few of the activities that are handled routinely by contract personnel. Although their various duties and responsibilities are also mentioned within the context of the rodeo events, below is a brief description of what some of these indispensable helpers do.

RODEO SECRETARIES, always capable and efficient, ensure that order does not quickly revert to chaos. They are the backbone of every performance, delving into their many tasks the moment a schedule is announced and heading home only after the lights go out. They are responsible for organizing the contestants and rearranging their often complicated timetables, for assigning the stock to competitors, keeping and recording times and scores, calculating results, and making sure everyone gets paid. Many rodeo secretaries bring a lifetime of experience and care for the sport, having been involved since their college years, or having grown up in ranching families. Some have handled receipts and proceeds from area livestock sales, or made their way to this sport through other means. Every contestant knows who the good secretaries are, appreciates their sometimes wry sense of humor, and counts on their honesty and perseverance.

STOCK CONTRACTORS provide rodeos with the necessary equipment, roughstock (the bucking horses and bulls), and timed event cattle (the calves and steers used for roping or wrestling). They also supply the horses used by rodeo queens or parade officials. Because so many timed event cattle are required, a stock contractor often buys or leases these animals instead of raising them. Roughstock, however, are always a long-term investment for the contractor. His competitive business revolves around buying, breeding, raising, and supplying top quality bucking horses and bulls to rodeos all over the country.

THE FLANKMAN works for the stock contractor and is responsible for placing and adjusting the flank straps on horses and bulls when they are in the chutes. He might also be asked to pull this strap tight when the chute opens. Proper adjustment of a flank strap is not often noticed by the audience, but it can influence the way an animal bucks.

LABORERS work in and around the arena to make sure the ground is well-prepared, the corrals, pens, chutes, and gates are set up and working properly, and that all of the animals are where they're supposed to be. A rodeo could not function without the aid of these experienced and interested helpers.

THE CHUTE BOSS is essential for a smooth-running rodeo. He makes sure that all roughstock are ready, and that the riders know their sequence. If a bull or bronc acts up, or if a cowboy isn't quite prepared to ride, the chute boss decides who will go. A good judge of men and animals, this person is always concerned for the welfare of the rider and horse or bull. He remains in constant contact with the judges and announcers to inform them of any changes or delays.

THE TIMED EVENT BOSS is responsible for overseeing the health and safety of the timed event cattle when they are in the holding pens. He has to get them prepared, lined up in the proper sequence, moved through the chutes, and ready to go. He also fosters communication between contestants, judges, and announcers, and keeps each event rolling.

Experience in understanding and handling cattle is absolutely essential in order to do this job well, because all calves and steers have different personality quirks. Organizing these bovines without agitating them makes it possible for every competitor to have a fair and equal chance to succeed in his event.

Other contract personnel look out for the safety of competitors and animals:

MEDICAL PERSONNEL supply much-needed aid. Perhaps more than any other sport, rodeo inflicts on its competitors a constant array of injuries requiring immediate or long-term care: crushed bones, torn ligaments, severe lacerations, dislocations, joint injuries, and bruises. Every rodeo is well-equipped with public or private emergency medicine technicians and professionals to treat the cowboys. The Texas-based Justin Boot Company sponsors a group of specialists called the Justin Sportsmedicine Team. Their mobile unit helps out six thousand cowboys at over 125 rodeos a year. Nicknamed the Justin Heelers, these physicians know almost every rodeo cowboy on a first-name basis—along with his list of injuries. And

THE PICKUP MEN HAVE SANDWICHED THIS BRONC IN BETWEEN THEM TO GIVE
RYAN MAPSTON A CHANCE TO GRAB ON AND PUSH AWAY FROM HIS HORSE.

THE PICKUP MAN HAS PULLED THE HORSE CLOSE TO HIM SO HE CAN RELEASE THE SHEEPSKIN-LINED BUCK STRAP. THIS NECESSARY TASK CAN BE DANGEROUS AT TIMES, BECAUSE SOME BRONCS CONTINUE BUCKING AND WILL KICK OUT AT ANYTHING NEARBY, INCLUDING ANOTHER HORSE.

they are quite familiar with stiff upper-lipped types who acknowledge no pain yet are glad to know that expert help is immediately available. According to the Team's reports, bull riding produces the largest number of injuries, followed closely by bareback riding.

THE RODEO VETERINARIANS are specialists, trained to deliver immediate care to bulls, wild horses, and cattle. Fortunately, animal injuries are usually few and inconsequential: a pulled tendon, a bruised hoof, a bite from a pen mate. Should something more serious occur, however, the veterinarians are ready to provide expert medical care.

PICKUP MEN and their string of well-trained horses provide crucial help in the arena during the bareback and saddle bronc events, and occasionally during bull riding. Usually two riders are hired, although this can vary according to the size of the arena. These men are top horsemen, usually former rodeo cowboys, who know the events well and can sense when to step in and help. Combining strength, horse handling, timing, and roping ability, these men are critical to the health and safety of every athlete—cowboy and animal. They travel all over the country to rodeos with four or five of their best stock horses in tow. And although they are not well paid for

JOE BAUMGARTNER TRIES EVERY TRICK HE CAN, EVEN PULLING THE BULL'S
TAIL, TO MAKE IT TURN AWAY FROM A DOWNED RIDER.

their talents and responsibilities, the love of the sport and the way of life it represents keeps them going.

Their first job is to protect the rider, providing a place to grab on and push away from his bronc after an eight-second ride, and to make sure he is out of danger. Sometimes, if a cowboy gets a hand or foot caught in his equipment, the pickup men will rope the bronc and pull it closer in order to help out. Once the contestant is free and safe, the pickup men will turn their focus toward the bronc. First, the flank strap needs to be released, and if the horse is wearing a halter

PUTTING A HAND ON THE BULL'S HEAD IS A DARING BUT VERY DIRECT METHOD FOR GETTING ITS ATTENTION SO THE RIDER CAN RUN FOR SAFETY. THE BULLFIGHTER IS WORKING HARD TO PROTECT THIS COWBOY, TRUSTING THAT TIMING AND ATHLETICISM WILL BE ENOUGH TO ESCAPE INJURY.

and rope, called a "bronc rein," the pickup men will catch it so the horse doesn't step on it and get hurt. They then guide the horse to the exit, where it is unsaddled. During the bull riding event, both pickup men stay far from the action because their horses might divert the bull's attention. But they are available if a bull can't find the exit, sometimes roping those that need to be ushered from the arena.

Pickup horses are sturdy, extremely well-broke, and are unafraid of moving in close to a galloping, bucking bronc or towing a 2,000-pound bull out of the arena. They are more than just good, reliable roping horses. They need to be unflappable, ready and able to work under all conditions, regardless of flying hooves and extra riders vaulting onto their backs before dropping to the ground. These horses are some of the best animals in the rodeo business.

THE BULLFIGHTERS AND CLOWNS have the daunting task of protecting bull riders, sometimes by stepping in and sacrificing their own safety in order to save a downed rider. They also make sure the events run smoothly and that the crowd is entertained. Aside

Texas bullfighters Donny Sparks and Greg Rumohr (in red) team up for a big event. Donny is from Texarkana and Greg hails from Rio Vista. Like all men in this profession, they are heavily depended upon when something goes awry. Their business is to understand behavior patterns, know the bulls, and be familiar with the tendencies of each rider.

from possessing humor and compassion, every man who works in this capacity is an athlete, an animal behaviorist, and a daredevil. Whether helping behind the chutes, in front of them, or out in the middle of a big arena, these men provide laughter at just the right moment—and protection for a cowboy who may be in serious danger.

All professional rodeos have two bullfighters. Big rodeos also employ a clown who works inside the arena for the entire performance. He jokes constantly with the announcer as if in an Abbott and Costello routine, dishing out bits of information and wry humor. He might bring along a particular specialty such as working on a trampoline or riding a motorcycle when there is a break between events. But this man's job becomes serious when bull riding begins. He and his big, heavily padded barrel are the only protection the bullfighters have in the arena—their only safe haven.

FAMOUS BULLFIGHTER AND CLOWN LEON COFFEE DEMONSTRATES HIS GOOD HUMOR AND ABILITY TO ENTERTAIN THE CROWD WHILE AWAITING MORE ACTION AT THE NATIONAL WESTERN STOCK SHOW IN DENVER.

The few men who choose this sport come from a variety of backgrounds and professions, but all are up for the challenge and have had a good deal of experience with cattle. Their careers might begin by helping on a ranch, working in a feed lot, or just being around rodeo. But in order to become proficient, they have to understand bulls extremely well. Schools and clinics dedicated to teaching bullfighting techniques are the best and easiest way to learn about bull behavior. The men who succeed in this business are fast on their feet and willing to put their lives on the line to save someone. Their makeup and funny clothes are for the audience, the bright colors help to distract a bull, and the padded knees and soccer shoes are for protection and speed.

Many of the contract bullfighters in rodeo also compete in their own series of events where they vie for prize money and reputation by challenging bulls and performing stunts that only daredevils would attempt. The bulls that are used in these special events are usually a breed called the Mexican Fighting Bull: smaller and much quicker than their bull riding counterparts, with a shorter fuse and a longer lifespan. In this competition, each man is given time alone in the arena with a bull. His goal is to stay as close as he can while showing his ability to take unbelievable risks. If he doesn't feel he's had enough after the required forty seconds, he can opt to continue for another thirty seconds. The sport is thrilling to watch—and the bulls are truly focused on a good fight.

ALL OFFICIAL JUDGES ARE SPONSORED BY WRANGLER.

Ensuring fair competition in rodeo are the judges and timers:

THE JUDGES work from the arena floor. In striped vests, and carrying red flags, these men have dedicated themselves to earning the title of Rodeo Official. They watch the cowboys and the livestock, decide whether the rules were followed or penalties incurred, and what score to award. From high school to professional levels, these officials know the rules inside and out. If judging a PRCA-sanctioned rodeo, they are required to attend annual seminars and stay current with rule updates or changes. Judges have to stay absolutely alert during every second of competition and then give their honest, immediate opinion of what they saw. There is no second guessing here . . . every paycheck earned is the result of their scores.

Two **TIMERS** hold the official stopwatches for every event except barrel racing, where they act as back-ups for an electronic timer. Working from the announcer's stand, timers carefully respond to what they see. They know the rules that determine when time should start and stop, and they also respond to the judges who flag each run from within the arena. Although the timers are neither seen nor recognized during a rodeo, every contestant depends upon their full attention and accuracy.

The final group of people categorized as contract personnel are those who reach out to the public, either by entertaining or by enlightening people about rodeo and what happens during each event:

RODEO ANNOUNCERS communicate the spectacle of rodeo to the audience. They know every aspect of the sport—from the history of a particular animal or cowboy to the way each one tends to perform. The announcer's job is to educate and amuse, to work magic with a crowd. When the microphone is on, this person is responsible for holding the entire rodeo together.

The primary announcer sits in a booth high above the bucking chutes where he can oversee the action in and around the arena. Sometimes, especially in the larger rodeos, a second announcer will work in the arena on horseback, wired with a microphone so he can communicate with other key players: secretaries, timers, chute bosses, stock

PRCA Announcer Will Rasmussen entertains the crowd from high above the arena floor. The good-willed Montana businessman travels all over the country to bring his wit and expertise to rodeo fans.

contractors, and clowns. A rodeo announcer must be fully prepared and knowledgeable about the bucking stock and certain horses or bulls that have earned reputations for being especially difficult to ride. He makes a point of knowing each of the cowboys, and is ready to weave stories about them into his banter whenever time permits. When there are problems or delays in the chute or in the arena, he can pick up the tempo with jokes and interesting sideline comments, often enlisting the help of the rodeo clown.

> *"My job is to announce the rodeo: what's happening in the arena at that particular moment in time, to educate the people who don't know much about the sport, and to entertain the people that do."*
>
> —Will Rasmussen
> Choteau, Montana

ENTERTAINERS provide diversion for the crowd during big rodeos, with a halftime show that usually involves skilled animals. There are trick riders and ropers, horses, monkeys, or dogs that perform amazing stunts. A herding dog, for instance, might demonstrate its ability to round up cattle, or the majestic Budweiser Clydesdales may grace a big arena while the announcer describes their place in western history. Sometimes, precision riding groups or western bands perform, many of whom are amateurs traveling at their own expense to share a special part of western heritage with the crowd.

RODEO QUEENS are the ambassadors of this sport and an ever-present sight at performances throughout our country. They are excellent horsewomen, cowgirls, and athletes who have edged out their competitors to earn the year-long title of Miss Rodeo for their home state. Ranging in age from eighteen to twenty-four, these women travel all over North America and abroad to promote rodeo and to honor our western way of life. They face a daily regimen that is often filled with back-to-back media interviews, riding demonstrations, and photo or autograph sessions. During every rodeo performance these young women carry the country and state flags, help to herd cattle toward the exit during the timed events, and are available to answer questions from the fans. Rodeo Queens work hard to present rodeo and rodeo animals in a realistic and positive fashion to the public.

RANDY SCHMUTZ OF STEPHENSVILLE, TEXAS, WORKS FROM HORSEBACK.

Before a rodeo begins, the arena is buzzing with activity, although much of it is invisible to the arriving crowd as they are ushered through to public parking, ticket booths, and concession stands.

PREVIOUS PAGES: READY TO ANSWER QUESTIONS FROM RODEO FANS, CARRY THE STATE FLAGS, AND HERD EACH OF THE TIMED EVENT CATTLE TOWARD THE EXIT ARE TARA GRAHAM, MISS RODEO AMERICA 2001, AND KRISTY MENSIK.

From seats overlooking the arena, however, the view reveals an array of preparations:

※ A tractor must plow the arena floor with a disc or roller packer, sometimes spraying water afterwards to keep the dust down and to achieve the proper consistency. The soil should be a correct mix of sand and dirt, and must be plowed between some of the events in order to maintain a consistent depth that provides good footing. If the ground is too soft, too hard, too rocky, or too slippery, the horses and cattle won't perform to their potential and may even trip or fall, endangering themselves and the contestants.

A HOMETOWN PARADE INCLUDES MANY EQUESTRIANS WHO HAVE LEARNED HOW TO CARE FOR THEIR HORSES AND WANT TO BE A PART OF RODEO.

HELPING MOVE THE NEW ARRIVALS INTO SORTING PENS IS WELL-KNOWN PICKUP MAN FLINT HEMSTED, A KNOWLEDGEABLE COWBOY WHO KNOWS HOW TO HANDLE ANIMALS SO THEY DON'T GET SCARED OR STRESSED.

❄ Over to one side of the rodeo grounds is a temporary village of horse trailers that have been organized in some sort of workable fashion and topped with bales of hay to feed the valuable equine travel partners of the timed event contestants. Ranging from new aluminum models with air-conditioned living quarters to beat-up ones that can barely get down the road, these trailers are owned by men and women of steel, inside and out, who are here to rodeo. If they don't do well, they are quickly back on the road and headed for a performance in Greeley, Fort Worth, Livingston, or Calgary—always moving toward another opportunity to win.

❄ Semi trucks filled with rodeo stock have come and gone over the past few days. If one is in sight, pulled up near one end of the arena, it's there to unload cattle or horses that have come from a nearby source. These late arrivals will be quickly

sorted and herded into pens so they'll have time to settle down before the rodeo begins. Most of the stock are housed in pens under and behind the bleachers that overlook the chutes. Although the public rarely gets close to the roughstock, most of these animals are easy to spot from the bleachers.

❋ Various rodeo personnel are visible, especially those helping out near the end of the arena where the timed events are staged. Someone will be putting horn wraps on the steers to protect them from rope burns while another counts and organizes cattle; one or two judges are usually checking the chute gates and the barrier rope, and measuring the time line, while someone else sets up the electronic eye for barrel racing.

❋ Contestants roll in unannounced and generally unnoticed, heading first for the rodeo office to pay

27

entry fees and then toward their private areas behind the chutes. They all know the schedule of events and the order in which they will ride. Normally, the sequence begins with bareback and ends with bull riding, but all of the cowboys know ahead of time what to expect. Roughstock riders usually arrive with traveling partners and friends a few hours before the performance, hefting gear bags and saddles. They take their time getting ready, changing into favorite clothes, visiting, stretching, looking over the stock and their equipment, taping arms, and protecting old injuries. The media is always nearby, wired for interviews and

SADDLE BRONC RIDER JOHN HAMMACK IS DISCUSSING LEG EXTENSION WITH STOCK CONTRACTOR IKE SANKEY. A SLIGHT ADJUSTMENT TO STIRRUP LENGTH CAN CHANGE THE WAY A RIDER USES HIS LEGS AND FEET.

THE PEOPLE RESPONSIBLE FOR ORGANIZING AND HANDLING THE EVENTS ARE TRADITIONALLY RECOGNIZED DURING THE GRAND PARADE, A WONDERFUL OVERTURE TO MANY RODEOS.

looking for a story or two, but none of the cowboys seem to be distracted. Timed event competitors are not as easy to spot until just before their event begins. Most are out by their trailers or temporary stalls, readying horses and gearing up for competition.

❋ The stock contractor and his helpers will have already prepared and sorted their animals, and lined up the necessary roughstock equipment, but you can still find them in the arena—they're the ones answering everyone's questions. A contractor might be found behind the chutes talking to a saddle bronc rider about a particular horse, and the next minute he'll be over at the end of the arena checking the order for steers. If an onlooker knows who to watch for, this man is interesting to follow throughout the entire rodeo—he's usually, though not always, wearing a starched white shirt.

As performance time approaches, everyone is gearing up for the grand parade. At the staging area, people of all types convene on horseback to honor a tradition that is often embellished with wonderful pomp and circumstance. Some parades include local children who have the honor of bringing in cattle for the timed events, while others feature dignitaries, sponsors, personnel, and rodeo queens who have traveled far to be there. Excitement builds in the grandstands when the rodeo announcer begins his commentary—and pressure rises underneath the stands as the

bareback riders make their final preparations. While flags unfurl and these men and women make their way into the arena, the bareback horses move, unnoticed, into the chutes.

Western heritage is celebrated with parades, pageantry, and formal introductions of key players. When Miss Rodeo America or the State's rodeo queen makes her entrance at a gallop and circles the arena with our national flag held high, every fan seems to catch the spirit. When she slows to a stop, a hush falls over the crowd, and everyone stands for the traditional singing of "The Star-Spangled Banner." Cowboys making final preparations in the chutes for the first event also take a moment to place hats over hearts for this age-old tradition that heralds the beginning of every rodeo.

COLORADO NATIVE TARA GRAHAM WAS MISS RODEO AMERICA 2001. LIKE HER PREDECESSORS, TARA SPENT THE YEAR TRAVELING AROUND THE COUNTRY TO REPRESENT RODEO.

IKE SANKEY BRINGS IN HIS MARES AND THEIR NEW COLTS FROM WINTER PASTURE IN CODY, WYOMING.

Stock Contractors and the Livestock

BEFORE A RODEO begins, and throughout, there is one key player who, along with his costly four-legged investments, should be recognized and better understood. This is the person responsible for orchestrating every event and supplying animals that are good enough to come to rodeo.

Over eighty licensed stock contractors in the United States and Canada are needed to provide professional rodeos with bucking broncs, parade horses, bulls, steers, and calves. This competitive business encompasses breeding and raising livestock, contracting with rodeos to provide quality animals for each event, and constantly overseeing their treatment. It is a year-round occupation that goes unrecognized outside the rodeo world, yet without good stock, a rodeo and all of its contestants suffer.

Raising and Preparing

Although the cattle used in timed events are bought and sold throughout the year, most stock contractors selectively breed their own roughstock, and supplement the

AFTER WORK IS DONE, THIS PROUD SADDLE BRONC MARE IS JOINED BY HER FOAL FOR A LAP AROUND THE ARENA. WITH HEAD HIGH AND NOSTRILS FLARING, SHE TRANSFERS A FEARLESS ATTITUDE TO HER OFFSPRING.

program by buying or breeding to outside stock. This is a long and expensive process, embraced only by those who know rodeo and who are willing to specialize in raising the best animals possible. It takes at least three years for a contractor to determine whether a young horse or bull will be capable of bucking. If temperament and build are right, it stays in the stock program. But it may take three more years to find out if that animal is of rodeo caliber. During this time, horses and bulls are "tried out" at home, usually by one of the ranch hands, and then "bucked" at a local rodeo or two to test their ability. If they show talent, they'll go to a few more rodeos. It is a long trial period, during which the stock contractor must provide food, water, veterinary care, pens, and a lot of rangeland for his maturing stock.

Even though these young, potential bucking animals are allowed to remain relatively wild and unbroken, a good contractor will make sure that they become accustomed to crowds and noise, chutes and pens, trucks and travel. He knows his bucking stock will fare much better without extra stress, and he prepares them accordingly. If a mare in his bucking string has a colt by her side, for example, the pair will be included in a few trips to rodeos close to home, and her baby will learn by example. Otherwise, new bulls or horses will acclimate by

A FUTURE ROUGH-STOCK CHAMPION WITH HIS MOTHER, SHEEP WAGON.

IKE SANKEY OVERSEES HIS BRONCS IN ACTION FROM A SEAT ON TOP OF THE BUCKING CHUTES.

AT AGE 23, SHEEP DIP (RIGHT), WILL LIVE OUT THE REST OF HER LIFE ON GOOD PASTURE AT THE SANKEY RANCH. KEEPING HER COMPANY IS ANOTHER BROODMARE NAMED CLASSIC, MOTHER OF THE FAMOUS SKITSO.

being exposed to things as a group, much like children.

Ike Sankey from Cody, Wyoming, and Joliet, Montana, has built a reputable breeding program with a stud named Custer and a mare named Sheep Dip. These foundation broncs were tough and well built—and they loved to buck. Custer is now buried on the Sankey ranch in Cody, and Sheep Dip, now twenty-three, has long retired from foaling. Their progeny dominate a large portion of the rodeo circuit. Sankey himself is a former bareback and saddle bronc rider, and he knows his horses. He and his wife, Roberta, have spent many years establishing a herd with good bucking bloodlines, healthy feet and legs, and outstanding athletic ability. The broncs and bulls on his two ranches have ample room to run free, so their hooves stay in good condition and their bodies remain physically fit.

The lush, rolling countryside south of Redding, California, is home to Growney Brothers Rodeo—famous for producing quality bucking bulls. John Growney is now concentrating on bucking

MARES AND THEIR COLTS ARE BROUGHT IN FROM PASTURE IN THE SPRING TO BE VACCINATED AND
CHECKED OVER. THEY WILL BE BRED TO SPECIFIC STALLIONS AND THEN EITHER TURNED OUT AGAIN
OR KEPT CLOSER TO HOME IF THEY ARE PART OF THE BUCKING STRING. PREGNANT MARES IN GOOD
CONDITION CAN SAFELY BE BUCKED FOR A FEW MONTHS.

horses, trying to build a reputation equal to that of his bulls. "We want our horses to get used to
all of the noises and moving around when they are still babies so they aren't stressed when it comes
time for bucking. People don't know how attached we can get to our stock." John tries to accustom
as many of his young horses as possible to wearing halters with long lead ropes. If they get used to
bending their necks and giving in to the rope when they step on it, they're less likely to hurt themselves later on when a saddle bronc rider drops his rope at the end of a ride.

Stock Identification

A contractor's reputation depends upon the health and performance of the animals he sends to rodeo. His roughstock and timed-event cattle are easily identified by their brand numbers, ear tags, or numbers patched on to their flanks. In order for cowboys to compete on a level playing field, the contractor is expected to supply timed-event cattle that are fresh and relatively even in weight, size, and temperament. For the roughstock events, he must always provide horses and bulls in top physical condition that want to buck. If he fails to produce quality stock, contestants will avoid entering the rodeos he contracts to—and the audience will suffer.

MATURE BRONCS LIVE A PRETTY GOOD LIFE AT THE GROWNEY RANCH BECAUSE THEY DON'T HAVE TO TRAVEL VERY FAR. QUITE OFTEN, THEY ARE ROUNDED UP, TRANSPORTED, BUCKED, AND RETURNED HOME WITHIN A MATTER OF DAYS.

Use and Longevity

With good care and management, a stock contractor can expect to see his superstar horses still delighting rodeo fans at the age of twenty-five. Bulls have shorter life spans, however, and can only buck until they are seven or eight. Rodeo roughstock exert a tremendous amount of energy in the few seconds they perform. As a result, they are "bucked" only once a day at the most, and somewhere between three and thirty times a year, depending upon the contractor and how he feels his animals are doing. Timed event cattle can handle a more rigorous schedule and are sometimes roped or wrestled more than once per day during a rodeo. But they are only useful until they decide not to run or until they grow too big for their event.

Sankey's bulls are escorted from pasture and put into pens in the same manner as his horses—though they tend to go at their own speed. There is never any "rodeoing" or shouting during a roundup because every good rancher or stock contractor knows how to work with his animals without getting them upset.

ROCK SPRINGS, WYOMING, IS HOME TO STEER WRESTLER SEAN MULLIGAN, ALTHOUGH HE SPENDS SOME OF EVERY YEAR ON THE ROAD. AS WITH MOST COWBOYS ON THE RODEO CIRCUIT, HORSES ARE VERY MUCH A PART OF HIS LIFE.

Animal Welfare

The first regulations guaranteeing proper treatment and protection of rodeo stock were put in place in 1947—seven years before the Humane Society was formed. Animal welfare is an important part of the sport of rodeo. Not only does it make economic sense to ensure the well-being of every rodeo animal, but the cowboys and contractors understand, care for, and depend upon them. A pen of healthy steers or calves, for example, costs a minimum of $10,000. Fairly solid broncs and bulls will cost about $4,000, whereas "superstars" can be worth upwards of $30,000. A reputable stock contractor needs to keep every one of his animals healthy and as free from stress as possible, or he won't stay in business very long.

Preparing for a Rodeo

Whether a contractor raises his own timed-event cattle as well as roughstock or finds outside sources to supply the calves and steers, he is still responsible for selecting, transporting, and feeding all of the stock at a rodeo. In addition, contractors often furnish the horses for rodeo queens and various dignitaries who ride in the parade, and might also bring along a spare

timed event horse in case one is needed. Providing animals for the various events requires a lot of planning. Not only must contractors supply halters, flank straps, and tack for the parade horses, they also have to prepare their animals for each trip. Bulls, at least a few times during the course of a year, must get the tips of their horns clipped off to the diameter of a half dollar. While the uncomplicated procedure often involves only an inch or two, the results are invaluable—a sharp horn placed correctly can gore a cowboy. Broncs must be previously immunized, sorted, and checked over. Finally, all that is left is the loading and shipping.

Rodeo animals are familiar with travel. The trucks used today for bucking stock have two levels with areas that can be sectioned off for studs or other horses that require separation. The upper level, with ramp access, is taller and allows more headroom for the horses. The

JOHN GROWNEY'S BRONCS KNOW WHAT TO DO WHEN IT'S TIME TO LOAD UP. THEY HAVE BEEN THROUGH THE SAME ROUTINE SINCE THEY WERE BABIES.

lower "pot belly" section is reserved for the bulls. If shipping is done late in the spring or early summer, some of the mares with colts will come too—an easy and less stressful way to familiarize the young with rodeo life.

Arrival

Double-decker semi trucks coming from a distance arrive a day or two prior to a rodeo. Those bringing stock from close by will arrive early on performance day. The animals unload down big ramps and move into sorting pens where they are organized, fed, watered, and left to settle down. This process is always overseen by the watchful eye of a contractor. Not only does he care for his animals, he also knows that their welfare and health are directly linked to their performance. Their arrival is an entertaining sight, especially the horses. Many resemble schoolchildren going out to a new playground at lunchtime. Heads and tails are high, eyes are wide as nostrils inhale the newness of their surroundings. Horses are very social and it takes a while for them to check out new neighbors and reestablish their pecking order. Bulls, on the other hand, lumber into the pens in a much less demonstrative way. They either get along or they don't, and they are separated accordingly.

RIGHT: THESE ARRIVING BRONCS FEEL NO PARTICULAR EXCITEMENT AS THEY WALK DOWN THE ALLEYWAY BETWEEN PENS. BUT THEIR COUNTERPARTS TO THE LEFT ALL HAVE EARS POINTED FORWARD.

YEARLINGS AND TWO-YEAR-OLDS ARE BROUGHT IN FOR A HEALTH CHECK SEVERAL TIMES A YEAR. THIS WAY, THEY GET USED TO PEOPLE, PENS, AND DIFFERENT CONDITIONS—BUILDING BLOCKS FOR A HEALTHY LIFE AS PART OF RODEO ROUGHSTOCK.

Bucking Horses

Bucking horses are rarely purebreds, although their bloodlines mean a lot to someone who is running a serious breeding program. Many of the best stock today are a mix of Shire and Thoroughbred, or Percheron and Thoroughbred, combining the draft horse's size and sturdiness with Thoroughbred agility and speed. But any cross can work, and some very good rodeo broncs have come from people who were simply unable to train them for riding. A horse that is well-built and athletic, with good legs and healthy feet, needs only one other attribute: the desire to buck.

Horses are bred to buck just as bird dogs are bred for hunting and retrieving. After they've had time to grow up and develop, a stock contractor will try them out in small local rodeos or at the home ranch where a few hired hands offer their abilities. Those that show potential will remain in the contractor's program, and as they grow, they will travel more, entering PRCA events and adapting to the rodeo way of life. Some will be designated as saddle broncs and others for bareback, depending upon what the contractor thinks about their build and the way they move. Later on, many are alternated between the two events in order to keep their minds and reactions fresh. Although these horses are allowed to remain fairly wild throughout their careers, they are handled frequently and learn not to fear humans or travel.

Broncs in the bucking string are well cared for and assured of a fairly good life—far better than the forgotten and neglected backyard ponies that dot the countryside.

Bucking Bulls

Bulls have not been as extensively cultivated in breeding programs as horses have, primarily because they don't live as long. If a bull proves to be exceptional after five or six years on the rodeo circuit, he is often retired and put into a breeding program. But then it takes another few years to know whether his offspring will be any good for rodeo. By then, it is less likely that the bull will still be able to produce. Still, there are some phenomenal bulls working today, many of which can be traced back to a bull named Oscar. Those that are world-class will likely be matched up with pro riders who belong to either the PRCA or the PBR.

SOME BULLS GET ALONG . . .   . . . AND SOME BULLS DON'T

There are two types of bulls used in rodeo, but for very different purposes. The smaller and meaner Mexican fighting bull is the choice for bullfighting competitions. These events are rodeos unto themselves, where the best bullfighters in the country vie for prestige and money by demonstrating an uncanny ability to read and outsmart their four-legged foes. Standard rodeos, however, only feature bull riding. Bucking bulls are usually Brahma or Brahma cross, meaning that they have been mixed with another breed like Longhorn or Hereford. Some have humps over their shoulders, but all have horns and thick, loose hides that roll as they move. These animals are not only extremely crafty, they are quite sensitive. A bull can move an inch of his skin to flick off a fly, or refuse to eat because the hay is slightly different, or even change the way he bucks because of the arena footing. Even though a good stock contractor will make sure his bulls are happy, temperaments vary. Some are simply mean. Whether in the holding pen or out in the arena, a rank bull is always looking for a fight. Others can get along and are easy to be around. This type might stand against the side

of a pen waiting for a scratch from a passerby, or move easily through chutes and gates without trying to gore or trample whatever might be in the way. Regardless of demeanor, bucking bulls have lightning quick reactions and big horns that they know how to use.

Roughstock Events

Prior to each event, the horses and bulls are sorted again by the contractor and helpers. Names or brand numbers are called off, various gates open and close as each animal is matched and put in correct sequence with the contestant's "draw." Then they are moved through alleyways leading to the chutes. The process is organized and fluid so that there is a minimum of stress.

When bucking stock move into the chutes just before their event, people are bustling everywhere—and so is the stock contractor. Although cowboy and animal both know the routine, decisions must be made, advice given, and equipment put on. The contractor might be telling a cowboy about a particular bronc's style while simultaneously trying to fish a cinch strap under a horse's belly. He could pull a bronc's flank strap tight when a chute opens, then quickly turn around and help unhook another rider's spur that's become caught in the rails. Or he might be using sign language to warn helpers and bullfighters in the arena that the bull in chute five will explode out of the gate with a hard turn to the left. Whatever the stock contractor is doing, or wants done, his leadership is well-respected.

After each ride, the contractor and personnel make sure that the stock are cared for. Pickup men maneuver their horses close enough to the broncs to remove the flank straps and herd them out of the arena. Bulls usually head for the open gate without any prodding. Once an animal is inside the holding pen, a helper checks it over, removes equipment, and sends it to another pen to be fed and watered. Timed-event cattle are also checked and sorted into pens where they settle down for the night.

Timed Events

A stock contractor who supplies timed event cattle has an array of breeds to choose from; the challenge lies in finding enough cattle that are uniform in size and temperament. The calves he provides must, by pro rodeo standards, be weaned from their mothers and weigh between 220 and 280 pounds. Steers need to have both horns and should weigh between 500 and 650 pounds. The contractor might be lucky and obtain cattle at a nearby breeding operation, or he may have to go as far as Mexico to obtain the necessary stock.

Roughstock Awards

At the end of every rodeo season, the top thirty PRCA cowboys from each event and the top fifteen bullfighters select and honor the best bucking stock. Contractors owning the animals receive awards and a halter for each winner with the animal's name inscribed on the nose band. A list of winners by year is included in the Appendix: Statistics and Records section, beginning page 235.

Introduction to the Events

THERE ARE SEVEN STANDARD EVENTS IN MOST rodeos today, divided into two categories: roughstock events which are scored by judges, and timed events in which the winners are determined by speed. The largest number of approved rodeos that include both roughstock and timed events in the United States and Canada are sanctioned by the Professional Rodeo Cowboys Association. The Women's Professional Rodeo Association (WPRA) governs competition specifically for women, and the Canadian Professional Rodeo Association (CPRA) sanctions the events in Canada.

A cowboy or cowgirl who wishes to compete as a professional must comply with the rules governing the association he or she wants to join. The PRCA, for example, requires a cowboy to be at least eighteen, meet certain requirements, and win over $1,000 in prize money at sanctioned events before he is allowed to purchase a Contestant Card that allows him to compete for year-end championships. Once he is a card-carrying member of the PRCA, he can only use winnings from a certain number of rodeos per year that count as official points toward year-end standings. Although the ruling on limits may change from year to year, riders who are trying to win enough money to qualify for circuit or world championships know they will constantly be on the road. Calling this "the suicide circuit," these cowboys often enter close to one hundred rodeos during the long season, driving or flying some 100,000 miles in pursuit of a berth at the prestigious Wrangler National Finals Rodeo in Las Vegas or at one of the other high-paying rodeos, which limit the number of contestants.

But the PRCA also offers an alternative that allows cowboys to stay closer to home, hold down a job, and still have the chance to earn a reputation and a lot of prize money. It's called the Circuit System, and a circuit cowboy can choose to compete in one of twelve geographic regions, winning money and earning points that count toward a championship event in that area. He can also apply these points toward the world standings and try to qualify for the Dodge National Finals Rodeo, which is held in Pocatello, Idaho, every spring.

ROUGHSTOCK events include bareback, saddle bronc, and bull riding. Each requires a cowboy to ride a bucking animal for eight seconds, holding on with only one hand. Roughstock riders usually team up with fellow competitors to travel between events, sometimes driving or flying to as many as four rodeos in a single weekend. All they need to bring along is their experience, equipment, and enough cash to make it to the next rodeo.

Judging is based equally on the rider's performance and that of the horse or bull. Two timers follow strict rules in determining when to start and stop their watches. Occasionally, timekeeping is backed up by a third judge who observes each run from behind the chutes. Two official judges watch the ride and determine their score from different locations in the arena. They stand to either side of the chute when the ride begins and then move around to get the best view as it progresses. Each judge can award up to fifty points: twenty-five for the rider and twenty-five for the animal. Much like scoring an ice skating or diving event, judges form a necessarily subjective opinion; but they know the rules and respond with extremely well-informed reactions.

A BAREBACK RIDER NOT ONLY NEEDS TO HAVE A GLOVE THAT FITS HIM PERFECTLY, BUT ONE THAT WORKS IN THE HANDLE OF HIS RIGGING. THE RIGHT FIT IS NOT ONLY KEY TO HIS RIDE, BUT TO HIS CONFIDENCE.

When judging the animal, officials look for its front-end movement, its power and reach, the way it drops down in front when kicking out, its rhythm and speed, and how hard it tries. In watching a rider, the judges award higher marks to someone who is in sync with his animal, has rhythm and timing, shows good leg and spurring action, and who can demonstrate he is willing to take risks while still maintaining control over his ride. For example, a great bronc or bull that works hard to throw its rider off will receive upwards of twenty points, twenty-five being a perfect score, from each judge. A cowboy who makes an exceptional attempt to stay aboard may also receive more than twenty points from each. In this case, a combined score from the two judges will be higher than eighty points—usually enough to earn a good-sized paycheck. However, in major rodeos like the National Finals, and those where entries are limited to only the top money-earning cowboys, combined scores in the middle eighties are more common.

Roughstock contestants in PRCA events enter rodeos and commit to paying the entry fees via a computerized central entry system called PROCOM,

which is located at PRCA headquarters in Colorado. These cowboys must do a lot of planning to organize their rodeo schedule. Figuring into their decisions are traveling partners, friends, or spouses, the location and proximity of each rodeo, the mode of transportation, jobs, recent injuries, and the quality of stock that will be supplied. Entry fees are determined by the amount of added purse money and sponsor contributions. Fees normally range between $25.00 and $125.00, but are much higher in rodeos where the added money is over $10,000.

Once the entry deadline passes, PROCOM determines the number of contestants for each event and notifies the stock contractor, who, in turn, calls back with names or identifying numbers of the stock he will provide. Then the "draw" that assigns rider to animal is made by computer and given to the rodeo secretary. Contestants can call a few days prior to a performance to find out their draw and decide whether they wish to compete. Unless a cowboy "draws out" due to injury, he will be expected to pay his entire entry fee before the event begins, regardless of whether he shows up.

TIMED EVENTS are a race against the clock. Each rider's goal is to post the fastest time without incurring penalties. The timed events included in most rodeos today are calf roping, steer wrestling, team roping, and women's barrel racing. Steer roping is another timed event, but it is included in very few rodeo schedules, partly due to time constraints. Because steer roping can also be tough on the animals and is not a recognized event in several states or in Canada, it will not be covered in this book. All of the timed events are staged at one end of the arena, and every contestant rides his or her own highly trained horse—or one that has been borrowed or leased from another cowboy.

Time is recorded by two stopwatches that are controlled by timers in the announcer's stand. Sometimes, a third timer will be hired as a back-up. The timers start and stop time in response to the flag judges in the arena. In barrel racing, an electronic eye is often used, but it is always backed up by a stopwatch. The timer's undivided attention is crucial to the outcome of every ride, and the cowboys have to trust that these individuals are dedicated to trying their hardest and that they want to do a good job. When each run is over, the barrier judge and field flag judges will assess any penalties by adding a predetermined number of seconds to the clock before the final time becomes official.

Timed event contestants enter PRCA rodeos in the same manner as roughstock cowboys, via the PROCOM computer system. But their commitment to their entry is even more definitive—scheduling plans can be very complex when one or two horses are part of the travel package. Additionally, ropers and steer wrestlers will not find out which animal they've been matched with until an hour before the rodeo begins, when the secretary draws names from a hat. Barrel racers, on the other hand, learn their riding order at least a week or two ahead of time

A TIMED EVENT.

so that they can plan further ahead. Timed event contestants often team up with fellow competitors who share similar goals. Together they decide which rodeos to enter, and rarely change plans midstream.

Entry fees for calf roping, steer wrestling and team roping range from $40.00 per person to $250.00, and barrel racers will pay between $54.00 and $514.00, again based on added purse money and sponsor contributions. As in roughstock events, when the added money is over $10,000, fees are set by the Event Representative and Director of Rodeo Administration.

In larger rodeos, there are often too many entrants in the timed events to fit into the constraints of a rodeo schedule. In order to accommodate the number of contestants, extra time, called "slack," is scheduled before or after the performances. Slack is a quieter time to compete, providing a more relaxed atmosphere for horse and rider to get to know the arena and the cattle. And if a contestant does well during slack time, he has a shot at winning his event. If not, there is ample time to pack up and head down the road to another scheduled rodeo.

Roughstock
Events

BULL: ONE /
BULLFIGHTER: ZIP

Equipment and Terms for Roughstock Events

ASIDE FROM A FAVORITE HAT, WELL-WORN JEANS, AND A clean, starched shirt, roughstock cowboys use specialized equipment made to fit their particular style and build. In most sports, highly prized equipment is new. But in rodeo, favorite equipment is often older, and well cared for over a long period of time. As cowboys develop their riding abilities, they find the right match in equipment and stick with it—same boots, same wrapping technique, same chaps, same spurs. Equipment, if totally new, could cost a saddle bronc rider over $2,000, a bareback cowboy about $1,500, and a bull rider up to $1,000.

BIND: A method for wrapping and securing the bull rope to the rider's hand.

BOOTS: Cowboy boots are designed to be light and pliable enough to enable a cowboy to easily move his legs and feet. He wraps a long leather thong around his boots to help keep them in place while spurring. Some roughstock riders choose to wear boots with a lower heel so that they can quickly get away from the hooves of a horse or the horns and legs of a 2,000-pound bull.

BUCK REIN: In saddle bronc riding, favorite buck reins are attached to the halters when the broncs come into the chutes. Where the cowboy decides to hold onto this rein is key to his balance. He uses his rope to measure the length of the bronc's neck, gathers information about the way it uses its head when bucking, and marks the place he will hold the rein when he climbs aboard.

A BAREBACK RIDER'S BOOTS AND SPURS NEED TO BE SECURED IN PLACE WITH A LEATHER THONG SO THEY WON'T COME OFF OR MOVE AROUND DURING QUICK SPURRING MOTION.

BULL ROPE: A bull rider uses a 16-foot flat braided rope made of manila, hemp, or polyester blend, with a handhold woven into it. The rider wraps the rope around the bull, pulls it tightly to the handhold, and then wraps the tail of it around his hand and fingers.

THESE BRONC SADDLES AND ROPE BUCK REINS HAVE BEEN SET DOWN BY THEIR OWNERS BEHIND THE CHUTES, WAITING FOR COMPETITION TO BEGIN.

BRONC SADDLE: A bronc saddle, originally designed in 1922 by a Canadian bareback rider and saddle maker named Earl Bascom, is made to fit each cowboy and his style of riding. The underside is lined with sheepskin and has a front and back cinch to help it to stay in place. These saddles do not have horns because bronc riders spend a lot of time in the air not knowing quite where they might sit down. The front swells are wide and rounded, and the cantle at the back of the seat is fairly deep, helping hold the cowboy in place. Bronc saddles have easy swinging stirrup leathers that sit further forward than on a normal saddle. They are made to facilitate the required back-and-forth leg motion while keeping both feet in the stirrups.

CHAPS: Leather leggings that roughstock riders wear for protection as well as decoration. They are fairly light in weight and designed specifically for each cowboy. The cut and texture is intended to help the cowboy's grip and accentuate his leg action without impeding spur contact or causing him to trip when he dismounts. Saddle bronc riders often rough up the insides of their chaps with a steel brush to help create more friction against the saddle.

CLOTHING: Pro Rodeo dress standards require every contestant to wear a cowboy hat, long-sleeved shirt with a collar, jeans, and boots. Roughstock riders bring along a duffel bag full of gear when they come to a rodeo. Most of these cowboys wear clothing and boots that advertise brand names, and their shirts and vest and chaps are covered with enough sponsors' logos and patches to rival stock car racers. Although they appear to bask in financial support, rodeo cowboys receive very little in the way of outside funding. They do not enjoy the many benefits allotted to other professional athletes.

DRAW: A random selection, made via computer or rodeo secretary, that matches a stock animal with a contestant and assigns the order in which he will compete.

FACE GUARD: Some bull riders, especially those who have been seriously injured in the past, choose to wear face guards similar to those worn by ice-hockey goalies.

FLANK STRAP: Also called a "buck strap," it is similar to a nylon or leather belt. It fits around the animal's flank, behind where the back cinch of a saddle would be. Even though rodeo horses and bulls are bred to buck, they become street-smart and often need this extra cinch to nudge them to do their eight-second best. Like other rodeo equipment, flank straps must meet Pro Rodeo requirements that protect the animals. All straps must have a quickrelease mechanism that is easy to reach from horseback or on foot. Straps used on broncs are lined with sheepskin because horses' hides are thinner than those of bulls. The stock contractor or his flankman know just how tight to pull each strap—each animal is slightly different. The strap should be tight enough to stay on but loose enough that the animal thinks he can kick it off. If a flank strap is too tight, the animal will simply not want to buck.

GLOVES: Bareback and bull riders need to protect their riding hand with a fitted leather glove. Each glove is hand-sewn and designed to suit the cowboy's particular needs:

> ❋ A bareback rider relies heavily on his glove and the way he can wedge his hand tightly into the handhold of his rigging. The glove is made of dense leather with an extra layer in the palm. A

SHAWN SHILD MAKES CUSTOM BAREBACK GLOVES FOR A CLIENT IN THE BACK ROOM OF HIS BLACKFOOT, IDAHO, TACK SHOP. KNOWN ALL OVER THE WORLD FOR HIS LEATHER WORK, HE MAKES EVERYTHING FROM SADDLES TO CHAPS AND SPECIALIZED GLOVES.

leather thong wrapped around the wrist helps prevent it from moving. He jams this glove so snugly into the handhold that sometimes he has difficulty getting it free once the ride is over.

✳ A bull rider wears a thin leather glove made of deer skin on his riding hand for both protection and grip. The only thing that keeps the rope secured around a bull when it's bucking is the cowboy's grip—if his glove slips, it may signal an early trip to the ground. These riders like a fairly new glove that fits snugly, so they can feel their hold on the rope.

HALTER: Saddle broncs are always haltered so that the buck rein can be attached. A stock contractor might also use a halter on a bareback horse if he feels it will make the

bronc drop his head and buck better. Halters usually have the stock contractor's brand engraved on the leather, and some of the most outstanding broncs in a bucking string receive special halters with their names engraved across the nosepiece. Canadian broncs that have bucked at the Calgary Stampede wear halters sporting their names.

HELPER: A fellow competitor or friend who lends a hand while a contestant is getting ready to ride. Roughstock cowboys look out for each other and are ready and willing to step in and help when someone needs assistance. A helper might calm a horse, adjust the rigging, pull a cinch under a bronc, or hold a bull rider's torso while he is leaning over to tighten his rope. This camaraderie among opponents is one of the many examples of fine sportsmanship in rodeo.

HIGH ROLLER: A bronc that leaps high in the air when bucking.

BILLY ETBAUER TIGHTENS HIS CINCH WHILE OTHER HELPERS MAKE SURE EVERYTHING IS IN ORDER. IN THE BACKGROUND, STOCK CONTRACTOR JOHN GROWNEY ADJUSTS THE FLANK STRAP.

MARK OUT (ALSO CALLED "SPUR OUT"): In bareback and saddle bronc events, a rider must have both spurs placed over the point of the horse's shoulders before it takes its first steps into the arena.

MULEY: A bull that does not have horns.

QUICK RELEASE: A specially designed buckle attached to the flank strap, that, when pulled, instantly releases the strap.

RAKE: Rolling a spur along the horse's hide is called raking. This spurring action is required of bareback and saddle bronc riders. Raking will not cut an animal's hide because the rowels of a spur are blunted and about ⅛-inch thick. A horse hide is five millimeters thick and the hide of a bull is about seven millimeters thick.

RE-RIDE: An opportunity awarded by the judge for a roughstock rider to have another chance to compete if his first ride was hampered by something not under his control. A re-ride might be awarded when an animal falls, does not buck to its potential, or if equipment supplied by the stock contractor breaks.

RIGGING: A bareback rider uses his rigging to keep connected to the horse. Rigging is essentially a leather and rawhide handle sewn and riveted to a wide piece of sole leather. D-rings attach the rigging to a latigo strap and wide cinch that wraps around the horse's belly. The style of this important piece of equipment has changed considerably since the turn of the century when bareback riding was first introduced into the rodeo arena. The one-handed rigging used today was designed in 1924 by Earl Bascom. Considering the incredible whipping motion of a good bucking bronc, simply holding on is not enough to keep connected—handles are custom-made to fit each cowboy's grip and allow only enough room to wedge his glove into position.

ROUGHSTOCK: Bucking horses or bulls in rodeo. All roughstock are considered to be athletes by the cowboys; and at the end of every year, top animals in every rodeo event receive special awards from various associations.

ROWELS: Blunted, star-shaped wheels at the end of the spur shank. They are at least ⅛-inch thick, and dulled at the points to satisfy Pro Rodeo guidelines, and prevent an animal's hide from being hurt.

✵ Bareback and saddle bronc riders use rowels that spin loosely and roll along the sides of a horse, helping the cowboy to show off his leg movement without hurting the animal.

✵ Bull riders use a dull, loosely locked, five-point rowel that moves only about a quarter of a turn. These riders need to be able to grab onto a bull's thick, loose, and rolling hide. Getting this grip is crucial to staying aboard.

SHANK: A piece of metal that connects the spur to the rowel. Shanks vary in length, curve, and slant, depending on the size of a cowboy and his preference. Changing the shank to fit a cowboy's build started when an all-around cowboy from Colorado figured out that he could stay in contact with a horse's hide more easily if he turned the shank inward. Paul "Shanks" Carney promptly won the world bareback riding title, changing the way shanks have been designed ever since.

✵ Bareback riders use spurs with longer shanks (about two inches) so they can reach higher and further forward, to the neck or shoulder. This length allows for more "drag" pressure and resistance, and helps the rider keep in rhythm and stay in contact with the horse.

A BAREBACK RIDER'S SPURS.

❋ Saddle bronc riders use a shorter shank. These cowboys must spur from the horse's shoulder to the back of the saddle (the cantle) and avoid catching a spur in the latigo, leather cinch, or buck rein during this rapid motion.

❋ Bull riders use a long shank (2-2¼ inches) that is often curved inward to help the rider have a better chance of maintaining contact with his bull.

SHIN GUARD: Some saddle bronc riders wear shin guards to keep the top of the stirrups from bruising their shins.

SPINNER: A bull that spins continuously in either direction. Spinners are not as hard to ride as bulls that combine their spin with bucking.

SPUR OUT: see **MARK OUT**

TAPE, BRACES, VESTS: Protective gear is essential to a cowboy who wants the chance to beat the odds. Padded vests, wraps, and neck padding are commonplace in roughstock events now. The vests are fairly flexible, with special padding over the sternum and a belt that helps bind the abdomen and support the back. Neck collars can be attached to those vests, further protecting the spine from whiplash.

✳ Bareback riders are a chiropractor's dream: these cowboys take more physical abuse than a bull rider. A bareback rider puts tremendous physical stress on his riding arm. His back and neck are also subject to a "whipping" motion, as his only connection to the bronc is his handhold. Tape, bracing, and vests are common, especially for older and more seasoned cowboys—the more injuries they have endured, the more protection they need. Proper taping from hand to elbow is extremely important and requires practice. If a cowboy does not tape himself properly, he can cause an injury rather than prevent one. The tape runs from hand and wrist to somewhere above the elbow. It is thickest underneath the forearm, where the cowboy's arm is leveraged against his hipbone. Those with chronic elbow problems also wear a brace over the tape to further protect this easily injured joint.

✳ Saddle bronc riders use their riding arm to hold onto the rope that is attached to the bronc's halter. To ensure some form of protection from the give-and-take motions that a bronc demands, they often tape their arms in a fashion similar to the way a bareback rider does, though allowing more flex. Many of these cowboys wear vests and neck braces.

✳ Bull riders need every kind of protection available. Thicker protective vests are a must in this event. Since there is no easy way off of a bull, neck braces are often added, and face guards are becoming more popular. These cowboys also tape their riding wrist in a way that allows for rotation and turn as they get snapped around on the bull.

WELL, WELLING, OR IN THE WELL: When a bull starts spinning, it can force the rider in toward the center of that spin—the "well"—putting him into an extremely dangerous position. A bull will intentionally keep a spin going if it feels the rider is losing his balance, which is why a bullfighter will step in and attempt to change that pattern by distracting it.

Bareback Riding

UNLIKE MANY RODEO EVENTS THAT STEM FROM EVERYDAY work on the range, bareback competition had its start in the arena. This event is known to be the most physically demanding in all of rodeo—an incredible test of arm strength, balance, and spurring action matched with the bucking abilities of a horse. The cowboy strives to stay aboard for the required eight seconds.

To do this, he depends upon the snug fit of his hand in the rigging, because a bronc's up-and-down movements can create a whipping motion that throws him in every direction. With his free hand in the air, the cowboy tries to synchronize his movements with the horse, rolling his spurs from the front of the shoulders up to the handhold while trying to impress the judges with his ability to control a wild ride. Scoring is based equally on the performance of horse and rider—the better the performance of the cowboy and the harder a horse bucks, the higher the score.

Background Preparation

Most cowboys who ride the powerful bucking horses in pro rodeo have had years of experience. Their ages may vary from eighteen to somewhere past forty, but frequent shoulder and elbow injuries take a serious toll. Most often these riders start as youngsters in high school, with ranch life in their background. They join associations that teach the basics and give them some exposure to different types of horses. Those that feel they have potential continue at the collegiate level and compete on a rodeo team, an invaluable way to build experience. Outside help from pros around the country is always available, as are rodeo schools that offer three-day or week-long teaching clinics. In addition, there are many small rodeos and other opportunities for a young cowboy to ride a variety of broncs. It takes a good deal of practice to learn to fit a glove in the handhold of the rigging, to know how to get aboard, start out of the chute, use a spur, and ride all types of horses. These cowboys must also learn the different ways of dismounting—and know what to do if their hand gets caught in the rigging. There is a

HAVING QUALIFIED SEVENTEEN TIMES FOR THE NATIONAL FINALS RODEO, CLINT COREY, FROM POWELL BUTTE, OREGON, IS ONE OF THE MOST CONSISTENT RIDERS ON THE CIRCUIT.

"right" time to sit forward and unwedge a glove jammed into the handhold; there is a certain way to lean sideways and grab on to a pickup man while in the process of pushing away from the bronc; there is a method to avoid being trampled if bucked off but still caught in the rigging; and there are several ways to buffer a fall and hit the ground softly.

Kelly Wardell grew up around horses in Wyoming. "When it came time to go out and earn a living, it was either go to work in the oil fields or rodeo; so I chose rodeo and have never looked back. I'm almost forty now and hope to continue riding for another few years. I have friends all over the world because of this sport." Kelly is the PRCA bareback riding contestant representative and selects horses for some of the top rodeos.

LARRY SANDVICK TAKES THE TIME TO STRETCH OUT HIS LEG MUSCLES BEFORE THE UPCOMING RIDE.

He has completed sixteen seasons as a professional and led the world in bareback earnings for the entire 2001 rodeo season. He also earned a berth on the 2002 Olympic Command Performance Rodeo team along with his travel partners, Rocky Steagall and Lan LaJeunesse, where each won a medal.

Once a bareback rider has satisfied PRCA requirements that allow him to compete as a full professional, he has to decide where his talents can take him and how much time he can commit to a career riding broncs. Whether staying near home to compete on the regional circuit or going for broke and making rodeo a full-time occupation, his experience, dedication, physical stamina, and attitude are the keys to future success. If he's not always able to be on the back of a horse, he will find the time to work on physical conditioning and spurring technique.

When a cowboy pays his entry fee, he usually knows who is supplying the bucking stock, who the pickup men will be, and what the rodeo grounds are like. A few days before the event, once he's learned which bronc he is to ride, he'll make a decision based on his draw and weigh traveling expenses against his potential for winning. If he knows the horse from prior experience or reputation, his choice will be easier. Otherwise, he learns as much as he can from the stock contractor or other contestants: the way the bronc comes out of the chute, how it bucks, if it twists and turns or moves straight, and whether he feels the horse is good enough to allow him a chance to win some money. Most likely, he will decide to go to the rodeo and take his chances.

Arrival at the Rodeo

Bareback competition is always the first event, and riders usually assemble behind the chutes a few hours before a performance so there is ample time to look over the horses and make physical and mental preparations. Comfortable jeans replace the starched and creased Wranglers typically worn by every cowboy, riggings and gloves are checked, boots secured with leather thongs, and chaps buckled on. Then comes all of the protective gear. Wrists, arms, and elbows need to be taped in a very particular fashion, vests and neck braces

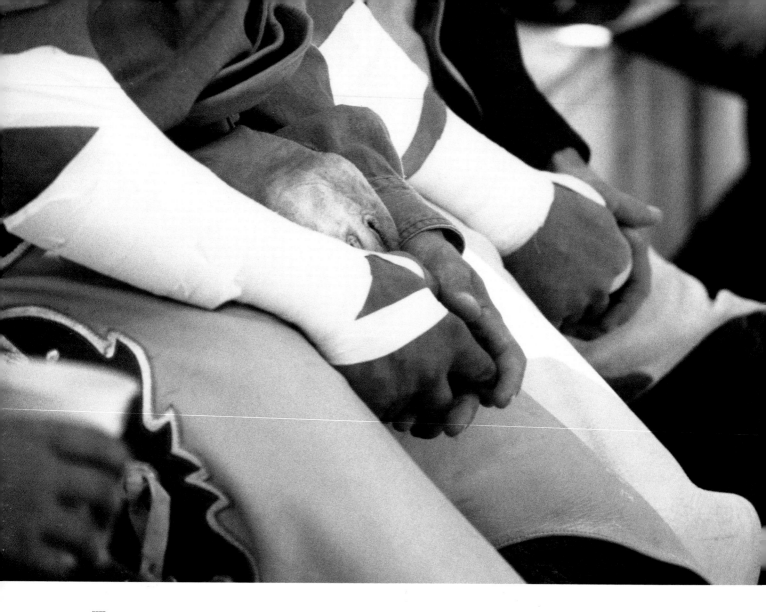

WRAPPED AND WAITING, THESE COWBOYS SIT ON THE PLATFORM BEHIND THE BUCKING CHUTES WHILE THEY LISTEN FOR THE RATTLE OF GATES.

put on, gloves wrapped tightly to the wrist. Sometimes these cowboys are able to make their preparations in private behind the chutes, but often TV cameramen and reporters are hovering around looking for interviews or photo opportunities.

Clint Corey knew that he wanted to rodeo at the age of seven and began a long and lucrative career after finishing high school. He is proud that he can make a living and support his family by doing what he loves. He tells people that he is getting close to retirement, but every year after a grueling ten days of National Finals Rodeo competition, he decides to come back—"just for one more year." Of his successes, Clint says: "You've got to be prepared and consistent in all you do, to take care of your body and equipment, and try to do things right every single time you ride." Clint was the 1991 world bareback riding champion, won the Wrangler NFR bareback average title in 2001, and competed in the 2002 Olympic Command Performance Rodeo, held just outside Salt Lake City.

Every bronc rider and helper moves into action with the sound of horses moving into the chutes. This unmistakable rustle trumpets the start of rodeo and sends a big rush of adrenaline through everyone close by. The cowboys move across a narrow band of wooden planks behind the chutes in order to reach their assigned horses. With the help of fellow competitors, each rider fits the rigging loosely onto his bronc. Some of the horses will stand perfectly still, seemingly docile while rigging is adjusted. Others act up, snorting and kicking the sides of the chute. Either way, once the rigging is in place, the contestants usually move away to stretch their muscles and try to relax while the rodeo announcer builds anticipation and prepares the crowd for "The Star-Spangled Banner". Bareback riding commences the moment the music stops and everyone has cleared the arena.

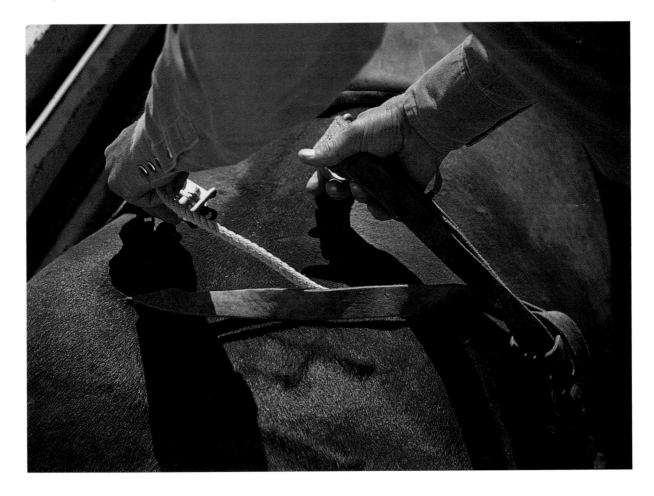

THE STOCK CONTRACTOR IS RESPONSIBLE FOR PLACING FLANK STRAPS ON EVERY HORSE WHEN IT COMES INTO THE CHUTE. THE STRAPS ARE LINED WITH SHEEPSKIN SO THAT THE LEATHER DOESN'T HURT A HORSE'S HIDE.

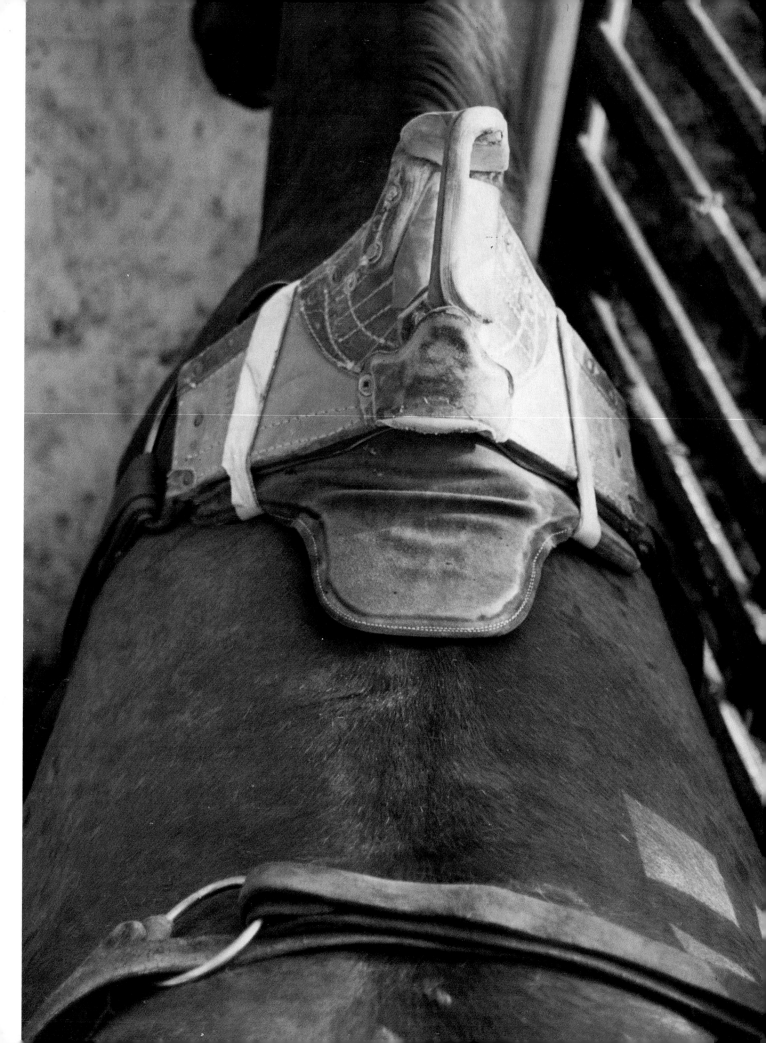

Ready

Just before the cowboy is scheduled to ride, he returns to his horse with a few people he has asked to help—usually fellow competitors or traveling companions. Being in the chutes and preparing to ride is a dangerous time for the cowboy, and every helper is acutely aware of this. Anyone involved knows horse behavior and will do whatever is necessary to help a contestant or settle down a nervous or stubborn bronc.

The rigging's placement and adjustment affects the way a horse bucks and how a cowboy rides. It has to sit on a horse's back just behind the shoulder muscle and then be tightened down enough that it will not move. If it's at all loose, a cowboy will be thrown around unnecessarily. Should it slip, both horse and contestant could be injured.

With a signal from the chute boss, the rider climbs down onto his bronc, cocking his body slightly to the side so he can get free if the horse leans on him or acts up by rearing or trying to lie down—broncs are crafty and will try to psych out their rider while he is trying to sit down and fit his glove into the rigging. With someone ready to pull him to safety at a moment's notice, the cowboy then works each finger through the handhold. His riding hand has to be snug almost to the point of being stuck, because grip itself is not enough to keep a bareback cowboy connected to 1,200 pounds of bucking horse.

The cowboy now assumes the position that will be the foundation for his ride. He scoots his hips and tailbone up

EVERYONE APPEARS TO BE SET, ESPECIALLY THE BRONC THAT HAS COCKED ITS BODY AGAINST THE SIDE OF THE CHUTE—AND KELLY WARDELL'S LEFT LEG. THE STOCK CONTRACTOR AND LAN LAJEUNESSE WAIT, READY TO DISTRACT THE HORSE JUST ENOUGH THAT KELLY CAN REPOSITION HIS FOOT AND NOD FOR THE GATE TO BE OPENED.

close to the handle of the rigging, lifts up hard on that handle, squares his shoulders, curls his body slightly, and tucks his chin down to his chest. Then he raises his free arm in the air and nods his head at the official to open the gate. The instant there is any room in the chute, even before the horse has turned to buck, the cowboy sets his spurs evenly and firmly in the trough of the horse's neck. As the gate opens, the stock contractor pulls the flank strap tight—tight enough that it will stay in place but loose enough that a horse thinks there is a chance of kicking it off.

The Mark Out

Judging begins the moment the chute opens and the bronc steps into the arena. On that very first jump, if the rider fails to keep both spurs set over and above the point of the horse's shoulders when its front feet hit the ground the first time, his ride is essentially over. No matter how spectacular the remaining seconds, missing the "mark out" or "spur out" means instant disqualification and is the cause of many a cowboy losing a big paycheck. The mark out rule is

NEITHER HORSE NOR RIDER SHOULD WAIT LONGER THAN NECESSARY TO GET ON WITH COMPETITION. HERE, THE HELPERS ARE TRYING TO SETTLE THE BRONCS DOWN WHILE RIDERS MAKE LAST MINUTE ADJUSTMENTS.

designed to give the bronc a slight advantage when it starts into the arena—a cowboy who has his legs extended forward, with toes pointed out and spurs set solidly against the horse, is not exactly in a balanced position. A horse can feel this imbalance, and it encourages him to buck harder.

The mark out is not always easy to see. Two judges are standing close enough to the chutes to watch carefully for it, but they can't always see each spur clearly on a bronc that twists as it lunges forward. If there is a question about the mark out, and a third judge is

SCOTT JOHNSTON SHOWS HOW WILLING HE IS TO TAKE EXTRA RISK ON THIS HORSE BY USING A TECHNIQUE CALLED FLOATING, OR LAYING WAY BACK AND APPEARING AS IF HE IS GOING TO BE BUCKED OFF. HE IS ALMOST DARING HIS BRONC TO BUCK HARDER.

watching from behind the chutes, the primary judges will look to him for a thumbs up or thumbs down. Understanding the difficulty of judging this critical rule, a cowboy often holds his spurs in place for more than one step or jump in an effort to make sure the officials see. But a seasoned bronc often has its own way of fouling up the best of plans. It may pause for a moment, creating just the slightest hint of apprehension for its rider and cause further imbalance, or it may simply explode out of the chute and leave the rider unable to keep his feet in position.

STOCK CONTRACTOR RENO ROSSER TIGHTENS THE FLANK STRAP ON HIS GRAY BRONC WHILE DEB GREENOUGH LAYS BACK AND SETS HIS SPURS FOR A PERFECT MARK OUT.

The Eight-Second Ride

A bareback bronc can go anywhere he wants in an arena. He is the leader in this eight-second dance, and if he is good at his job, he will do everything he can to buck off a rider. Conversely, the cowboy has to show the two judges that he can match the rhythm of this horse and anticipate its every move, wherever it chooses to go. It's horse against man, and man against horse—with the judges carefully watching the efforts of both. Every time a bronc's front feet hit the ground, the bareback rider pulls up hard on the rigging and tries to extend both legs forward to the horse's shoulders, with toes out so that the judges can clearly see the placement of his spurs. A split second later, as the horse winds up for another kick, the cowboy must draw his legs and spurs clear up to the rigging handle, bending his knees so that they almost hit his chest. His free arm, which must not come in contact with anything for risk of disqualification, stays in the air and is used solely for balance. A bareback rider is constantly trying to synchronize his movements with the horse's, while attempting to impress the judges at the same time. He knows he needs to make every second count.

The mechanics of riding are complicated, and the more seasoned and confident the cowboy, the better able he is to adapt to each horse. While spurring rhythm, balance, and other technical aspects remain the foundation of bareback riding, styles differ widely. Some cowboys maintain more of an upright position while others lie far back on the horse and ride wildly, flinging their upper

CLINT COREY RIDES A HIGH ROLLER NAMED CROW.

CODY JESSE DEMONSTRATES CONSIDERABLE ABILITY ON A DIFFICULT BRONC. ON THIS JUMP, HE HAS PLACED HIS SPURS EVENLY AND CORRECTLY OVER THE SHOULDER BEFORE THE BRONC'S FRONT FEET HAVE HIT THE GROUND.

bodies in every direction. This latter technique is a more modern style, and often a good way to show the judges how much risk a rider is willing to take. But there are disadvantages. Whenever the rider's backbone is not in line with the horse's, he may be unable to place his spurs evenly and exactly where he wants—a technicality all judges watch for. However the cowboy chooses to ride, though, he stays on, keeping his hips close to his rigging, and relying on balance and arm strength.

Dismounting

From amateur to professional, all roughstock cowboys are practiced in ways of getting free of their animals. Whether they've become caught up in the rigging or are just trying to latch onto one of the pickup men, they have to know how to get out of a bad situation, stay clear of the bronc's hooves, and land safely. If a cowboy manages to stay on his horse until the eight-second whistle, he immediately tries to sit up and forward, almost curling his body over the horse's withers to absorb the bucking motion while he works his hand free of the rigging. Then he makes a choice: bail out and take his chances on landing a safe distance away, or wait for the pickup men to move in and help.

ANOTHER HIGH ROLLER DOING EVERYTHING IT CAN TO TOSS THIS COWBOY AT THE NATIONAL WESTERN STOCK SHOW IN DENVER. THE JANUARY SHOW IS ONE OF THE OLDEST, LONGEST RUNNING RODEOS IN AMERICA AND HERALDS THE BEGINNING OF RODEO SEASON.

The pickup men—if they are good at their job—provide contestants with a sense of security during a very dangerous time. Their first job is to move in close so the rider can grab on and get free from the bronc. When a rider's hand is caught in the rigging, the pickup men will release, or trip, the flank strap so the horse no longer tries to buck as hard. Then they'll sandwich the bronc between their horses in order to settle him down.

Getting bucked off with a hand still "hung up" is a serious situation and one that all roughstock riders rehearse for. Since a bareback rider wants to avoid being dragged, the safest thing to do is to stay as close as possible to the bronc and keep his feet on the ground. If this is possible, he can either try to keep working his hand free while the pickup men are moving in, or he can grab the horse's mane and leap back on, trick-riding style. In the meantime, the pickup men will work very hard to rope the horse and slow things down.

Sandwiched in by the pickup men, Pete Hawkins is having trouble working his hand free of the rigging. One of the pickup men has readied his rope in case the bronc needs to be controlled. Both Pete and Scott Johnson (see page 83) have both suffered broken backs and other serious injuries, but both are still going strong.

KEN CLABAUGH AND HIS HORSE PROVIDE AN IDEAL WAY FOR THIS RIDER TO GET TO THE GROUND.

Marvin Garret, from Belle Fourche, South Dakota, can ride well on just about any type of horse he encounters. His positive attitude has carried him through many serious injuries, including a broken back following a tragic plane crash. Marvin is clearly a leader in the bareback event and has won four world titles to show for it. His brother Mark is also highly respected in the sport as is their nephew, J. D. Garrett. Thoughtful and articulate, Marvin serves as a beacon to many young cowboys who are striving to learn from the pros. After many successful years, he explains the role a bronc plays in rodeo: "I remember telling someone recently that when you get to a certain level of competition, the riders are all really good, and it boils down to the horse you draw. You've got to be mounted or you're just not going to excel."

A bucking horse finishes its work when the rider and flank strap are gone. It is then herded into a holding area called the "stripping chute," where the rigging is taken off. From there, the bronc moves through an alleyway of metal panels into a big settling pen with other horses. Rodeo broncs know the routine well. They also know their job is done—for a week, or for a few months. A cowboy, on the other hand, finishes his work either by heading back to the chutes to help fellow contestants, or to the medical room to be treated for an injury. The only guaranteed outcome for every bareback rider is being very sore.

The Judges

As in other roughstock events, a very respectable score from two judges totals over eighty points, with 100 being perfect. If the rider succeeds in making a good, solid mark out, judges then look for an aggressive performance from both the cowboy and the bronc. A horse needs to be willing to buck hard and try every trick possible to toss its rider. The more difficult he is to ride, the better the judges react. A bareback rider must show ultimate confidence in his ability to ride and handle every situation. He might exaggerate the

RIDING WITH A VERY SORE ARM AND UNABLE TO FREE HIS GLOVE FROM THE HANDHOLD, KELLY WARDELL IS IN TROUBLE. HE HIT THE FENCE, WHICH WAS ENOUGH TO FREE HIS HAND, BUT HE ALSO RECEIVED A SIZEABLE HEAD LACERATION. EARLY THAT EVENING, HE AND HIS PARTNERS WERE BACK IN THEIR VAN AND HEADING FOR A RODEO IN GREELEY.

difficulty of his bronc by lying way back or to the side during each buck, but he also must continue spurring evenly and correctly with both feet.

The Horses

The stock contractor decides how often to "buck" each of his horses during the season, using criteria such as energy level and temperament, willingness to buck, arena conditions, and more. Some are used once a week during peak times while others will only be bucked a few times over the course of a year. Regardless of the number, the type of bronc everyone wants to draw has rhythm, kicks high, jumps straight, and works continuously to buck off a rider. The tough ones—the "eliminators"—are a bigger challenge because they buck inconsistently, change leads, duck, dive, and take huge, athletic jumps. If a rider can stay balanced and make it to the whistle on the back of an eliminator, he has a fairly good shot at winning his event.

Bareback horses are of all shapes, sizes, genders, and ages. Like their riders, the broncs have different personalities and styles of bucking, with reputations that follow them around the country. Some become superstars that every cowboy dreams of riding, sporting names like Jubilee, Eliminator, Happy Howard, Dirty Dan, Snake Pit, Roly Poly, and Nightmare. Skoal's Alley Ways is a bay gelding owned and raised by Kesler Championship Rodeo in Alberta, Canada. Though not a large horse, the power behind every one of his moves has taken many riders to championships. Cool Alley, another Kesler horse, was voted the 2001 Wrangler NFR top bareback bronc after successfully bucking off every contestant. Another top horse is Khadafy Skoal, owned by Powder River Rodeo, an older blue roan gelding that has been voted bareback horse of the year three times. And then there is the dark bay stallion that carried Mark Gomes to his first NFR championship. Owned and raised by Beutler and Gaylord Rodeo Company, Copenhagen Comotion gives every rider all he's got simply because he does not want anyone on his back.

Red Lodge, Montana, is home to a cowboy with a long list of family members involved in rodeo and a deep appreciation for horses. Deb Greenough remembers first trying to ride a bronc when he was

WHEN A RIDER IS HURT, ALL OF HIS BUDDIES AND FELLOW COMPETITORS ARE THERE TO MOVE IN TO HELP.

just a toddler. That particular backyard bronc happened to be a white propane tank. Deb retired from rodeo at the end of 2001, and is breaking and training horses full time while he raises a family. "Horses ought to be considered man's best friend. I treat a bronc standing in the chutes just as I treat my saddle horses—with utmost respect."

CODY,
WYOMING

Saddle Bronc Riding

KNOWN AS RODEO'S CLASSIC EVENT, SADDLE BRONC RIDING began in the early 1800s out on the wide-open ranges of the West. Rivalry was the natural result of the cowboy's competitive spirit, an extension of watching each other break wild horses for ranch work. Good horses were a necessity—as were cowboys who could stay on them long enough to introduce them to a life of working cattle.

Saddle bronc riding today closely resembles those early competitions. The cowboy sits deep in a hornless saddle, one hand grasping a thick, braided rope attached to the bronc's halter. He must stay on his horse for eight seconds without letting go of the rein or losing a stirrup, and he cannot touch any part of himself or the horse with his free arm.

This event is a competition of balance, timing, and fluid motion. As in bareback, the saddle bronc rider must first satisfy the "mark-out" rule, with both spurs stretched out forward and in contact with the horse's shoulders when the chute opens and he takes his first step into the arena, or he'll be disqualified. The cowboy then synchronizes his leg movements with the bronc's bucking motion, pulling on the rope rein to stay balanced and to maintain contact with the saddle. His leg and spurring motion is extremely technical because his heels and spurs must roll from the point of the horse's shoulders all the way back to the cantle at the rear of the saddle each time the horse bucks. This is difficult to do continuously without losing a stirrup or getting a spur caught in the buck rein or in one of the cinches.

Arrival and Preparation

Saddle bronc riders prepare just as other rodeo cowboys do—with years of practice. Although there are similarities between bareback and saddle bronc riding, there are also big differences. Spurring technique in both events requires the cowboy to turn his toes out so his heels and spurs can stay in contact with the horse. But the saddle bronc rider moves his legs

GLEN O'NEILL NOW CALLS WATER VALLEY, ALBERTA, HIS HOME. THE AUSTRALIAN HAS WON CHAMPIONSHIPS IN THREE COUNTRIES AND BEEN RANKED AMONG THE TOP BRONC RIDERS IN THE WORLD FOR THE LAST SIX YEARS. IN 2001, DURING THE ANNUAL WEEK-LONG FOURTH OF JULY RUN KNOWN AS "COWBOY CHRISTMAS," GLEN EARNED MORE THAN $25,000 IN A SIX-DAY PERIOD.

from front to back instead of front and upwards. Also, he uses his riding arm and thigh muscles differently than a bareback rider does. Strong thighs allow him to grip while he swings his feet from the horse's shoulder to the back part of the saddle. Although a glove is not needed for protection, his riding arm has to be strong enough to hold and lift up on the rope buck rein that connects the halter to the head of a 1,200-pound bronc.

These cowboys often travel together, usually arriving at the fair-grounds just before the rodeo starts and staying out of the way of bareback riders and other cowboys unless asked to help. Although physical and mental preparations are different for each cowboy, they all allow time for visiting, stretching, checking fittings, buck reins, spurs, and roughing up the saddle seat and the insides of their chaps to prevent sliding. Regardless of the intense competition between all riders

FINDING THE RIGHT PIECE OF EQUIPMENT IS EXTREMELY IMPORTANT TO A COWBOY. ONCE HE OWNS SOMETHING THAT SUITS HIM, HE WILL KEEP IT IN GOOD WORKING CONDITION FOR AS LONG AS POSSIBLE.

gunning for the prize money, these cowboys will do anything they can to ensure fair and equal opportunity among themselves. The one thing in abundance behind the chutes is camaraderie and kinship.

Ryan Mapston is a good example of a cowboy who can do what he loves to do—and make a living from it. "This is just the greatest life. I love the independent spirit that accompanies every rodeo cowboy. I can travel with good friends all over the country, help my competitors when they're in the chutes, and then go out and compete with them when it's my turn."

THIS BRONC RECEIVES A CALMING HAND FROM ONE OF THE MEN IN THE ARENA.

Ready

While the audience is watching another event at the end of the arena, saddle bronc horses move into chutes where they are haltered and saddled. The stock contractor, or one of his helpers, puts each flank strap and halter in place. The contestant then attaches a buck rein to the halter and puts his saddle onto the bronc's back, loosely securing the front and back cinches. Preparation time in the chutes can always be dangerous. Even though most rodeo broncs are accustomed to the procedure, there are always a few that will act up—it's their first real opportunity to psych out the foe. Other horses stand perfectly still while equipment gets adjusted, waiting until the gate opens for their chance to explode.

As riding time approaches, every bronc gets his cinch tightened and buck rein measured and marked. The front cinch of a

GETTING READY FOR HIS RIDE, MATT MARVEL USES A TUFT OF HORSE HAIR TO MARK WHERE HE WILL HOLD HIS BUCK REIN.

THE FLANKMAN, IN THIS CASE, A BULLFIGHTER NAMED JOE
BAUMGARTNER, IS MAKING A LAST ADJUSTMENT TO THE FLANK
STRAP WHILE THE RIDER GETS READY TO GO.

saddle has to be tight enough so it won't slide around; the back cinch serves to keep it in place, but is left looser so as not to irritate a horse around his mid-belly. Where a rider chooses to hold onto his rope buck rein is key to the entire ride, and his experience and knowledge about the bronc are big factors in this decision. He wants a fairly tight connection with his horse in order to help maintain leverage and balance, and will measure the rope and mark it according to the horse's neck length and style of bucking. Too much rein on a high-headed horse, for example, will cause a change in equilibrium (and confidence). Or, if the rider doesn't allow enough rein for a low-headed horse, he will be jerked forward every time the horse bucks and lose the ability to set his feet forward on the shoulders.

A cowboy won't climb down onto the back of his bronc until just before his turn. With helpers around him for protection, he becomes quiet and focused. Methodically, he grabs the spot he's marked on the rein and holds it taut while easing down into the saddle. Then he works each boot into the stirrups, hoping the bronc does not lean hard on a leg or rear up and mash

IMAGING IS A METHOD THAT MANY ATHLETES USE TO HELP PREPARE FOR COMPETITION. HERE, TODD HIPSAG REHEARSES HIS UPCOMING RIDE.

him against the fence. Wedging his boots forward toward the horse's shoulder, he hunkers down in the saddle, tucks his chin, lifts hard on the rein, and nods for the gate to open.

The Mark Out

Judging begins the moment the chute opens and the bronc steps out into the arena. As with bareback riding, the cowboy must first mark out. It's a task made more difficult should the bronc rear, or stall a moment before exploding—just long enough to catch the rider off guard with a lapse of concentration. Whatever the method of grand entry, a rider needs to wait, spurs set firmly in place, for the bronc to make its move.

Scott Johnston is a master at marking out. He grew up near the Australian Outback with his grandfather who rode broncs. Now he lives in Texas in order to make a better living in rodeo. Scott rides bareback as well as saddle broncs. He travels by car, with his wife Jane and their four children, to as many rodeos as he can. His road has not been easy, and everyone in the business knows the battles he has faced: from being completely broke, to visa problems, to several serious physical injuries, including a broken back suffered in a plane crash. Scott was on the brink of winning the world all-around championship title in 2000, but "bucked off" in the last round while cameras zoomed in on his disappointment. While he was still in the process of dusting off dirt and pride, a reporter holding a microphone asked how it felt to lose the coveted title.

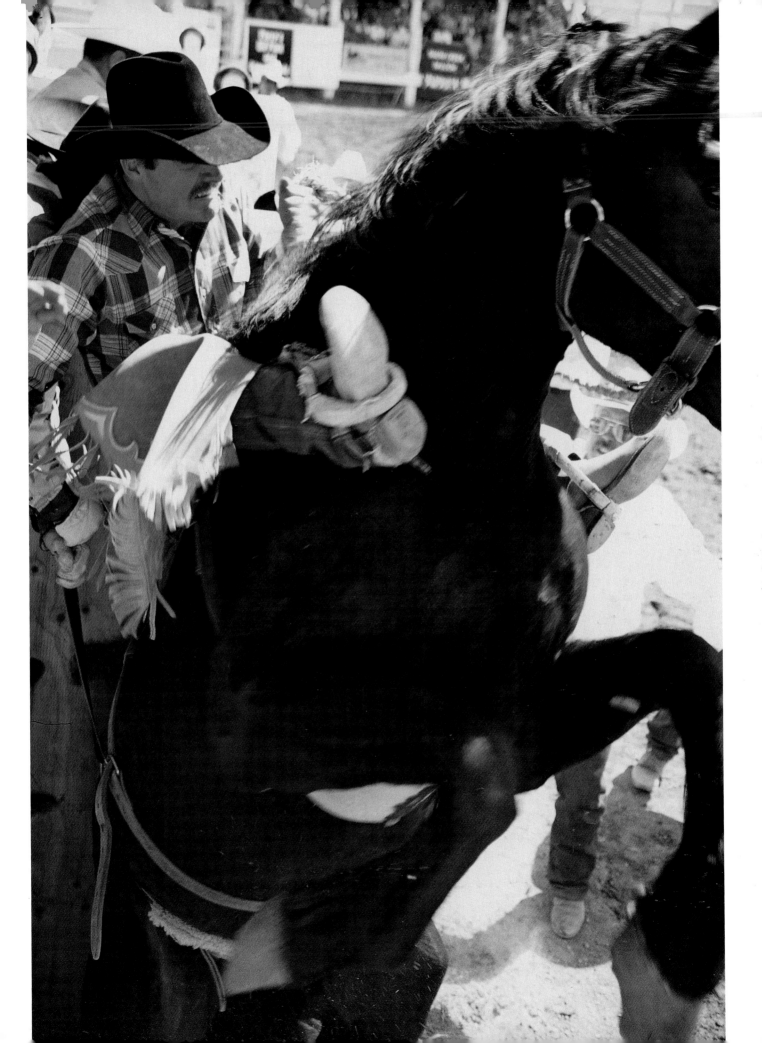

WORLD CHAMPION BILLY ETBAUER SHOWS THE BALANCE AND STYLE THAT HAS MADE HIM ONE OF THE FINEST AND MOST CONSISTENT RIDERS OF ALL TIME. HIS FEET ARE FULLY EXTENDED, WITH TOES TURNED OUT AND SPURS SET OVER THE SHOULDERS. NOT ONLY IS HE IN THE CORRECT POSITION, HE HAS GOTTEN THERE BEFORE HIS BRONC'S FRONT FEET HIT THE GROUND: A GOOD EXAMPLE OF HIS ABILITY TO ANTICIPATE.

Scott is still shaking his head from that one. But he is the type of person who maintains a positive attitude. "I guess I can say that my success has been pretty hard-earned. It's because I have a strong faith in God—but I also know how to work hard."

The Eight-Second Ride

Experience, body position, timing, and balance are crucial to a saddle bronc rider's perform-ance. To earn points from the judges, he has to be aggressive and extremely fast with his feet to stay in rhythm with the horse's bucking motion. He also has to keep his boots in the stirrups—heels down, toes turned out—in order to hold on with his calves and spurs. As for the upper body, balance is the key to staying on these exception-ally strong animals. A saddle bronc rider has to sit more upright than a bareback rider, partly to stay in the saddle, and partly because his legs swing back and forth, almost like a pendulum. The rider uses his free arm to counteract other motions and grips the buck rein as a leverage point. If he lifts up constantly on the rein, he has a better chance of staying down in the saddle and under the swell in front. When the horse kicks, he can use his hold on the rein to lean back, throwing his feet and spurs forward onto the horse's shoulders. Sometimes

WITH HIS RIDE ALMOST COMPLETE AND A PICKUP MAN MOVING IN TO HELP, JOHNNY HAMMACK HAS BOTH FEET POSITIONED CORRECTLY. HE HOLDS ONTO THE ROPE WITH HIS RIGHT HAND INSTEAD OF THE LEFT, WHICH CAN BE AN ADVANTAGE ON A BRONC THAT IS USED TO BEING PULLED BACK FROM THE RIGHT.

A GREAT DEMONSTRATION OF HOW FAR A COWBOY CAN MOVE HIS FEET BACK WHEN REACTING TO EACH JUMP. THIS POSITION IS HARD ON THE LEGS AND VERY DIFFICULT TO ACHIEVE BECAUSE THE RIDER'S UPPER BODY IS IN CONSTANT MOTION AS HE ADJUSTS TO WHAT THE BRONC IS DOING.

it's difficult to get both feet up and over the horse's shoulders, but his goal is to get them there before the bronc's front feet hit the ground. Then, when the horse jumps up and lunges, a hard lift on the rein and the forward reach of his free arm allow the cowboy to bend forward and move his boots clear back and up to the cantle.

Tom Reeves is a legend in rodeo with a consistent and perfect riding style. He did not have to qualify seventeen times for the NFR or win the 2001 World Championships to prove himself and his style of riding. "I'm proud that I can make a living and put together a home and family by following my

FAITH, SOUTH DAKOTA, IS HOME TO RED LEMMEL, A COWBOY EVERYONE SEEMS TO KNOW. RED IS IN A MID-AIR TRANSITION AND NOT YET FINISHED CHANGING POSITION IN THE SADDLE, SWINGING HIS FEET FORWARD TO THE BRONC'S SHOULDERS AS IT HEADS FOR THE GROUND.

GLEN O'NEILL CAN TAKE IN THE SCENERY WHILE HIS PICKUP MAN WORKS HARD TO MAKE THE EXIT A SAFE ONE.

dream. I guess you could say I've lived every part of rodeo. It has been a long, long road." Tom knew at age five that he would rodeo. His dream grew while he was breaking colts for his grandfather in South Dakota; he finished school while competing in various rodeos. After winning the world title, Reeves was quoted as telling a reporter: "I knew I had one bucking Jose (a bronc named Rodeo Houston) that belonged to my good friend Mike Cervi . . . I drew the one I needed. He was a bucking dude. If I'd had one of those little hoppers, I probably would have fallen off."

The Dismount

Whether ejected early or able to stay on long enough to plan a departure, every saddle bronc rider is not free from danger until he reaches the side of the arena. Even though these horses will not try to harm a person, they can do a lot of damage in a short amount of time with their hooves and heavy bodies. Pickup men are ready to help, but the rider has to prepare for many scenarios and be able to get to the ground in one piece. If he knows he is about to be bucked off, a saddle bronc rider automatically assesses the exit possibilities, kicks free of the stirrups, lets go of the rope, and lunges as far to one side as he can.

ROUGHSTOCK RIDERS HAVE PREPARED FOR VARIOUS EXITS, WHETHER VOLUNTARILY OR NOT. THIS COWBOY IS BAILING OUT AND ONLY HAS A MOMENT TO ADJUST AND SOFTEN THE IMPACT WHEN HE HITS THE GROUND.

AS SOON AS POSSIBLE, A PICKUP MAN WILL ATTEND TO THE BRONC. HE CAUGHT THE BUCK REIN TO PULL THE HORSE CLOSE AND HAS FLIPPED THE RELEASE MECHANISM ON THE FLANK STRAP.

THIS RIDER HAS
KICKED FREE OF HIS
STIRRUPS AND IS
USING THE HORSE'S
MOMENTUM TO GET
FURTHER AWAY. HE
WAITS UNTIL THE
VERY LAST MOMENT
TO LET LOOSE OF HIS
REIN.

He then tries to buffer the fall, avoiding a flat landing, so he can be on his feet as quickly as possible.

If the eight-second buzzer sounds, a cowboy normally grabs the buck rein with both hands, creating more leverage to prevent the horse from bucking as hard—a strong pull on the rein helps keep a bronc's head up. He evaluates the situation while kicking free of the stirrups. If he wants assistance from the pickup men, he will wait for one to get close enough and then grab onto the saddle or rider's torso while pushing away from his bronc. Should he decide to bail out on his own, he'll use the horse's bucking

Following a stellar performance at the National Finals Rodeo, Skitso spends the winter months with other special mares in a huge pasture near the Sankey home. The mares are rounded up in the spring for breeding, then selectively used throughout the summer. If the colt by her side is anything like his mother, he will become a prize bucking horse.

motion to help throw him farther away, holding onto the rein until the last possible moment so he has some degree of control over the bronc's direction.

Saddle Bronc Horses

Thanks to the excellent bucking bloodlines developed in breeding programs around the country, there are many great saddle broncs in rodeo today. With the addition of draft horse blood in the mix, these broncs are generally bigger and stronger than bareback horses, so they can easily carry the extra weight of a saddle, two cinches, a flank strap, and halter. And just like their bareback counterparts, they are bred to buck— they'll do anything to get rid of a rider. The really good ones, the superstars, never stop trying. The type of saddle bronc every rider hopes to draw is fast and strong, carries its head low, and spends time high in the air, either bucking or kicking with an even rhythm for the full eight seconds. The more difficult ones will leap, stumble, change direction, change rhythm, and toss their heads around. Some examples of tough broncs to ride are Skitso Skoal, Skoal's Wild Card, and Surprise Party. These three outstanding Custer-sired mares belong to Sankey Rodeo and have each earned a place in the record books. They have a reputation for bucking off some of the best riders in the world—and carrying others to record scores. Now, these mares spend part of the year raising colts at the Sankey ranch. Two-time World Champion Billy Etbauer said of an imminent date he had with Skitso at the NFR: "I've respected that horse for a long time. I told somebody it's a horse I can ride, but I don't know if I can ride her today." When commenting on his high scoring ride on Wild Card, Dan Mortensen said, "She is a perfect mold of what Ike's breeding program is about." There are many other great broncs around today, valued by stock contractor owners and recognized wherever they go. One notable mare, owned by Big Bend Rodeo, is named Spring Fling. She was voted top bareback bronc in 1997, carrying riders like Ty Murray, Deb Greenough, and Clint Corey to championships. She won top honors in 1999 as a saddle bronc horse, tied with Surprise Party for the top vote in 2000, and proved to be unrideable during the December 2001 Wrangler National Finals Rodeo.

Judging

Scoring in this event is the same as other roughstock events. Two judges each award up to twenty-five points for the performance of the rider and up to twenty-five for the performance of the horse. A total score of eighty is considered very respectable at most pro rodeos. At the 1999 National Finals Rodeo in Las Vegas, Billy Etbauer's winning score on the last night of competition was an all-time arena record of ninety.

Two judges stand on either side of the chute so they can see the beginning of the ride. Then they move around the arena, evaluating horse and rider. As horsemen, they have a good sense of where to be and understand the many ways a bronc tends to move; as judges, they know what to look for when assessing points. If the rodeo has a third judge standing behind the chutes, he holds a backup stopwatch and notes any penalties once the ride begins.

When the chute opens, the judges want to see a good strong entrance by the bronc, and a solid mark out by the rider. If the bronc should stall too long before entering the arena, judges might waive the mark-out rule, giving the rider what's known as a "free roll" for the start of his run. From there on, they look for an aggressive horse and rider who each demonstrate confidence and ability during the entire eight seconds. Judging stops at the sound of a buzzer or horn, and within seconds their scores are relayed to the announcer.

Judging is spontaneous and final. Sometimes, in lieu of a numeric score, the judges might declare a "no score" or a "re-ride." A rider who fails to mark out, touches his horse with his free hand, or loses his rein or stirrup receives a "no score." But if a horse did not buck to its ability, fell down, or if a contractor's equipment failed, the rider will be given an opportunity to ride another bronc after he has had a chance to regroup and catch his breath.

EVEN THOUGH THE BRONC CONTINUES TO PUT ON A FINE SHOW, TOM REEVES WILL RECEIVE A "RE-RIDE" FROM THE JUDGES BECAUSE THE BUCK STRAP CAME OFF. REEVES'S FLAWLESS STYLE HAS EARNED HIM A GREAT REPUTATION IN THE WORLD OF PRO RODEO.

Bull Riding

ODACIOUS, RED ROCK, DILLINGER, WOLFMAN, Promised Land, Locomotive Breath, Yellow Jacket, Wipe Out, Short Fuse, Rapid Fire, Barracuda, Titanic, Bad Mood, White Lightning, Woolly Bully, Cash, Trick or Treat, King Kong. Familiar names like these belong to the type of bull every rider hopes to encounter—and ride for eight seconds –during a rodeo career. The "eliminator" bulls have reputations for being some of the rankest and meanest—but their names mean big paychecks if a cowboy can stay aboard.

Who knows how this sport got started? Maybe it began with some young cowboys trying to ride calves in the back pasture. It became a rodeo event in the early 1890s when steers were used, but it wasn't an official bull-riding event until 1954, when a stock contractor named Andy Juaregui introduced Brahmas to the cowboys. Today, bull riding is rodeo's most popular event. It is certainly the most dangerous eight seconds of any professional sport in the world. Every time a bull rider climbs onto one of these tons-of-dynamite, he puts his life on the line. A fearless attitude and split-second reflexes are necessities, as are intense mental and physical preparations. A bull rider can only learn his trade by one method: riding a lot of bulls.

For a bull rider, the challenge is not only to stay on until the whistle blows, which is enough to be "in the money" at most rodeos, but to demonstrate that he is in control of his ride and in a position to defy his opponent. If he can maintain balance, stay in rhythm with the bull, and pique his ride by using an occasional spur, he will earn extra points. Just as in other roughstock events, his free arm cannot touch any part of the bull or he will be disqualified. He holds onto a flat, braided handhold woven into the bull rope cinch. The rider puts this rope around the bull, cinches it tight, and uses the tail of it to make a couple of wraps around his hand, securing it to the handhold. The rope will come loose whenever he releases his grip—unless his hand gets "hung up" in the wrap. Hanging at the other end of the rope is a three-by-six-inch copper bell. The bell serves two purposes: noise to make the bull even angrier, and extra weight to help the rope fall to the ground when the rider lets loose.

Bull riding is as solitary as it is dangerous, because the riders are pretty much on their own from the moment the chute opens until they reach the safety of a fence. They cannot be assisted by pickup men on horseback because bulls might charge a horse that comes in too close. But these cowboys do depend heavily on the two or three men on foot in the arena—the clowns and bullfighters who are experts in animal behavior and know how to use their cunning, skill, and athleticism to distract the bulls. Bullfighters often risk their lives, either in helping a rider stay on long enough to complete his ride, or by making sure he is safe from horns and hooves when he hits the ground.

Preparation

Bull riders have to ride all types of bulls in order to understand the behavior and movement of these extraordinarily quick animals. This is a sport for the young and daring, although there are a few who might reach middle age before retirement. Most young cowboys just starting out will attend special bull-riding schools where they learn how to maintain good body position and how to react to the array of moves a bull can make. By watching videos, riding mechanical bulls, and listening to the pros, they learn that fitness and technique will help their ride as well as their dismount. Then they ride as many bulls as they possibly can, quickly discovering that reaction time and strong back and leg muscles are imperative components for survival—they have to be ready to land hard, in every possible contortion, and get up to sprint for safety.

World Champion Gary Leffew offers very well-attended bull-riding schools at his ranch in California. His

FELIPE AARAGON, 1999 ROOKIE-OF-THE-YEAR, WORKS ROSIN INTO HIS BULL ROPE.

IF THE BULLFIGHTER CAN CATCH THE BULL'S ATTENTION AND SLOW IT DOWN, THIS COWBOY IS IN A GOOD POSITION TO GET HIS HAND FREE.

advertisement says it all: "When you're not practicing, remember . . . someone somewhere is practicing, and when you meet . . . they will win."

The mental preparation required to ride bulls is just as important as the physical. To stay on the rankest bull demands attitude and focus, with no room for doubt or distraction. Day after day of practice sharpens a cowboy's reaction time until his responses become automatic. Riders also learn how important it is to find a routine that suits them, and to stick with it day in and day out in order to block out peripheral distractions. Their focus has to remain on the task, uninterrupted by the excitement and adrenaline that accompanies the most dangerous rodeo event.

JUST AS IN
OTHER
ROUGHSTOCK
EVENTS, THE
BULL RIDERS
ORGANIZE THEIR
EQUIPMENT IN
A THOUGHTFUL
MANNER.

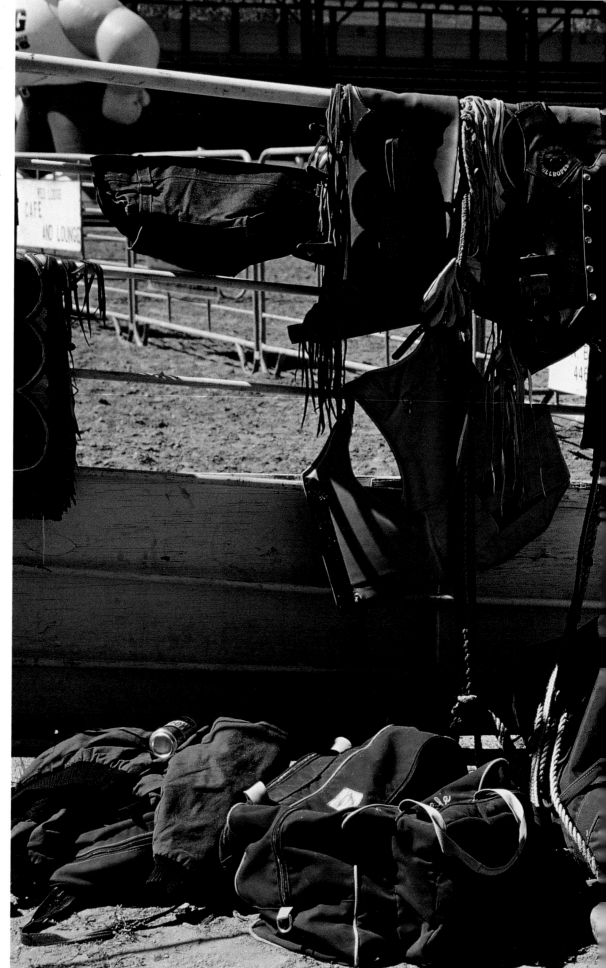

READY TO GO, THIS COWBOY WALKS TOWARD THE CHUTES
WITH HIS BULL ROPE AND BELL.

A BULL RIDER'S SPUR SHANK IS OFTEN CURVED
IN AND SOMEWHAT LONGER THAN THOSE USED
ON BRONCS, GIVING HIM BETTER CONTACT
WITH THE BULL. HE USES A LOOSELY LOCKED
ROWEL IN ORDER TO BE ABLE TO GRAB ON
INSTEAD OF ROLL.

Jesse Bail from Camp Crook, South Dakota, has learned how to ride bulls, and he is good at it. But he is young and incredibly versatile, eager and quite able to compete in other rodeo events such as saddle bronc and steer wrestling—and even team roping. He was a college all-around champion in 2000 and has won the prestigious Linderman Award twice for most versatile cowboy. "My father rode broncs and my mother ran barrels and trained horses. She's the one who taught me how to rope. I guess I had a pretty fair mix of things when I was growing up, and I'm lucky to be able to take what I've learned and rodeo professionally." Jesse chose a travel partner from South Dakota in 2001 who has given him some deep insight into rodeo and competition: World Champion Tom Reeves.

Arrival and Getting Ready

As bull riding is always the final event in a rodeo, a rider doesn't usually come to the rodeo grounds early enough to help other roughstock competitors or even to enjoy some of the rodeo. He walks in with one clear goal in mind, following his well-practiced routine so that nothing undermines his confidence. He usually hangs out with fellow competitors while making his preparations, often talking about something neutral, such as where he ate breakfast. A favorite pair of loose-fitting jeans replaces what he wore to the grounds; sometimes he puts on a different hat or a lucky shirt. Equipment is draped over a fence for inspection, and the bull rope receives an application of rosin. The

cowboy wraps his boots and spurs with a leather thong to keep them stationary when gripping the bull, and puts on his chaps. Taping comes next, but the technique is different from the way a bareback cowboy makes his wrap. A bull rider needs a lot of flexibility and will probably only tape his forearm.

Just before his ride, he puts on a snug-fitting protective vest that usually sports the logos of various sponsors. A neck brace is optional, although most riders want the added protection. Some cowboys also wear a face guard that resembles a hockey goalie's mask. Last to go on is the deerskin glove, which is firmly secured with tape or a leather thong. He rubs rosin on its palm to make it sticky—a good grip on the rope is his only chance of staying connected to the bull.

In the Chutes

Bulls are sorted and moved into the bucking chutes from holding pens while women's barrel racing is in progress. The sight and sound of these huge animals maneuvering their bodies and horned heads through the labyrinth of organized, narrow pathways brings a rush of adrenaline to the cowboys and helpers. Chutes rattle, gates slide open and slam closed, horns rake along the metal bars—the sensations are unmistakable to anyone nearby, but muffled for rodeo fans whose attention is directed elsewhere.

TO ROB BELL, A FORMER HOCKEY PLAYER FROM WATER VALLEY, ALBERTA, EVERYTHING IS QUIET AROUND HIM. HE IS INSIDE HIS OWN BUBBLE, IMMUNE FROM DISTRACTIONS. IN A MATTER OF MINUTES, CHUTE MEN AND HELPERS WILL SWARM AROUND HIM AS HE CLIMBS ONTO THE BACK OF HIS BULL. HIS FOCUS, HOWEVER, WILL REMAIN LOCKED ON THE TASK.

From a platform behind the chutes, bull riders and helpers put cinches and flank straps loosely around each bull, using long wires to fish the equipment underneath their bellies. Next, they look for a spot to get limber, focused, and psyched-up. They will stretch their arms, backs, and shoulders, or busy themselves by rewrapping their gloves and adjusting vests and neck guards. Some bull riders quietly focus inward, whereas others jump around, shadow boxing or slapping themselves to raise their heart rates. Regardless of their different rituals, no contestant steps into the chute until it's time to cinch up and go. A slight weight shift by the bull can crush a rider's leg against the fence; a lightning quick jerk of its horns could hook someone's head or arm. Chutes are no place for amateurs—or mistakes.

A HELPER PROTECTS THIS YOUNG COWBOY AS HE GETS SET TO MAKE HIS WRAP. THE MAN PULLING THE ROPE TIGHT WILL LAY IT ACROSS THE RIDER'S HAND AS SOON AS HE OPENS IT.

The process moves quickly when a rider is notified to get ready. With helpers standing by, he climbs over the rails and stands on the chute rungs to safely straddle his bull. He sits down, though further back from where he will ride so there is enough room to adjust his rope while staying clear of the horns. After he maneuvers his woven handle to where he wants it, a helper pulls the rope tight. Most

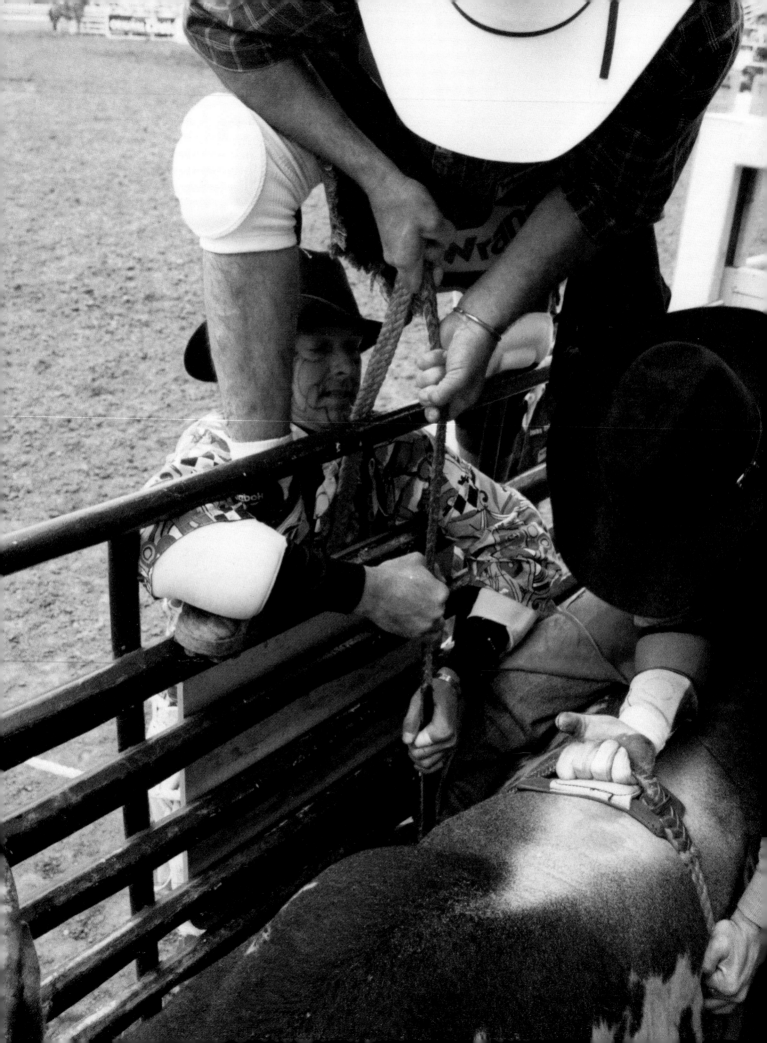

riders, whether left- or right-handed, set their handhold close to or directly over the bull's spine, near the withers and below the shoulder. Once the rope is pulled, a rider can repeat the process if he's not quite comfortable with the location, although the extra time might cause his hand to sweat—and a slippery glove can jeopardize his ride.

When a helper tightens the bull rope, he first pulls it straight up so that the rider can rub his hand up and down the area where he will make his "bind." Then the rope is laid across an open palm and the cowboy closes his fist over it to hold it in place. He takes this rope behind his wrist and lays it again across his palm, either flat or with a twist. Then he works each finger closed to make a tight fist. Some riders secure the rope further by pulling the end back between

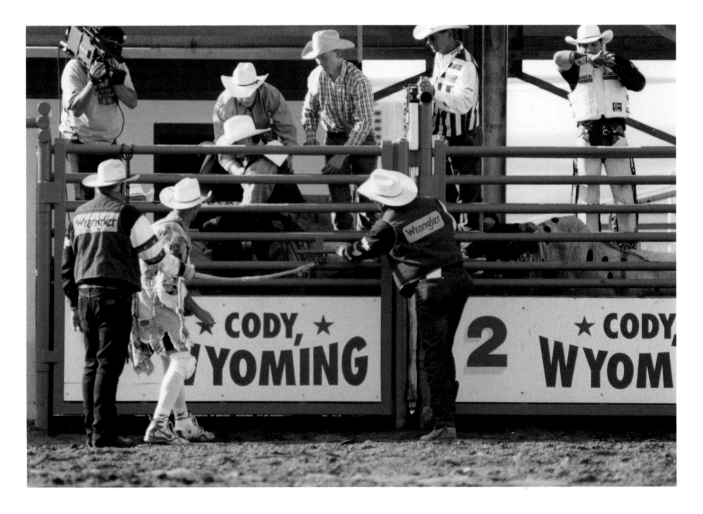

A BULL CAN HUNKER DOWN IN THE CHUTE ANY TIME IT WANTS. THIS CAN BE A DANGEROUS SITUATION IF THE RIDER HAS ALREADY MADE HIS WRAP AND SET HIS LEGS TO EITHER SIDE—WHICH HAPPENED HERE. EVERYONE AROUND IS READY TO HELP, WAITING FOR JUST THE RIGHT MOMENT TO EITHER GIVE HIM A LIFT OUT OF THE CHUTE OR OPEN THE GATE.

Rob Bell sits the bull evenly as it kicks and twists in an attempt to throw him forward where it can hook him with its horns. He keeps his legs low, using his free arm to counteract what the bull does. He is showing the judges that he is fully in charge of his ride.

their ring finger and pinkie, but this extra fold can get them hung up if they don't have time to undo it. Regardless of how a rider makes his bind, the intent is the same: to keep the grip as tight as possible and still be able to open the hand so the rope can fall loose.

The rider then positions himself squarely on the bull's back, wedges his feet and legs down a little further on each side, and scoots his hips up close to the handhold. He tucks his chin to his chest, raises his free arm in the air, and nods for the officials to open the gate—all in a matter of seconds.

The Ride

The beginning sets the tone for all that follows. Pro riders know that most bulls will try their hardest to buck a rider as soon as they have room, exploding out of the chute the moment it opens. Even if the cowboy has a pretty good idea of how his bull tends to move, he also knows that a seasoned and smart one can change behavior in a flash. Any panic or overreaction to the bull's moves can spell a quick end to the ride. If he is caught expecting his bull to come out of the chute spinning to the right and it lunges left instead, the rider has anticipated the wrong move, and any attempt to play catch-up will be futile. There is simply no room for error in bull riding. When the chute opens, the cowboy is completely on his own.

Cody Hancock climbed from fifteenth place in the world standings to win the World Championships in 2000. He has won several circuit championships as well, and is not at all ready

A COWBOY WHO CAN STAY CENTERED AND SNUGGED UP TO HIS HANDHOLD HAS AN EXCELLENT CHANCE OF STAYING ABOARD.

to slow down. The Taylor, Arizona, cowboy says *"Bull riding is the hardest sport in the world because it is a 145-pound. guy versus a 2,000-pound bull. You only get paid when you win, and I truly feel that the guy who tries the hardest will win the most. Even though a lot depends on the bull you've got, I try to win first every time I ride."*

Cody broke a long-standing PRCA and NFR record at the end of 2001 by scoring a ninety-six on Diamond G Rodeo Company's bull named Mr. USA. Prior to that, Don Gay and Mike White had shared the ninety-five-point record, in 1976 and 1999 respectively.

Bulls are always trying to move away from their rider and throw him off balance by spinning, bucking, or switching directions. If a cowboy is going to stay on, he needs to counter every

BULLFIGHTERS DISTRACT THE BULL SO THAT PETE ELKINS HAS AN EASIER SHOT AT FREEING HIS HAND FROM THE BULL ROPE.

action with split-second timing. He must avoid the inclination to anticipate what the bull will do, or make unnecessary movements that will jeopardize his balance. From the soles of his boots to the top of his free arm, he must constantly readjust his position in order to remain centered and in sync with the bull. He does this in several ways:

THIS BULL ADDS A SLIGHT TWIST TO A VERY HIGH KICK, TRYING TO THROW OKLAHOMA'S DANELL TIPTON FORWARD OVER ITS HORNS. DANELL SITS BACK, BUT NOT TOO FAR, SO THAT HE CAN GET IN A FEW LICKS WITH HIS SPUR.

❋ First, he concentrates his weight in each leg and uses quick footwork to find the right places to grab the loose and rolling hide. He knows that if his legs aren't down and his spurs aren't gripping when a big move comes, his entire balance is unstable.

❋ Second, he tries to stay in constant contact with the bull. This is accomplished by snugging up close to the handhold, lifting up hard on the bull rope, and using his free arm to counteract whatever the bull does. Were he to lean back and let his free arm also fall back as the bull ducks down in front, his legs would automatically be thrown forward and he would lose contact.

❋ Third, he wants to keep his torso centered and facing straight ahead, with shoulders bent slightly forward and his free arm up in the air. If a bull starts to

THIS COWBOY HAS BEEN TOSSED TO THE SIDE OF THE BULL OPPOSITE THE BULLFIGHTER. A DIFFICULT SITUATION, BUT A BULL CAN CHANGE ITS MIND IN A FLASH.

spin, it is usually trying to throw its rider to the outside. But if the cowboy overreacts, leaning inward, a bull can feel this and will force him further inside of his spin. Being caught "in the well" is a very dangerous situation. During a kick, when the bull ducks down in front, the rider needs to sit down hard and hold his free arm up and forward so he can't lean too far back. When the bull counters that motion and rears up in front, the rider also has to reach further forward, bending at the waist and reaching up between the horns with his free arm.

※ Fourth, he needs to keep focused on the bull's shoulder. It is an accepted maxim that if a cowboy isn't looking in the same direction the bull is going, he will end up landing where he was looking.

A bull rider can't out-muscle a bull. If he is to stay on for eight seconds, he has to use finesse. Then, to earn a high score, he has to use the bull's movement to his advantage and show that he can read and react to every move. This is called "riding the bull's momentum," or "staying with the bull." He also will try to dare the bull by spurring it—even just a few times—to show the judges he is willing to take extra risk in an already risky situation. Spurring is not a requirement, but it earns extra points, and can make up points on a bull that isn't bucking and trying its hardest.

The Dismount

Unless the cowboy can find the right moment to jump, there is no way to the ground other than by being ejected. This process can be relatively safe, but it can also be life-threatening. All bull riders are prepared, mentally and physically, for various scenarios—they know that danger is present as long as they are in the arena.

If the cowboy has any time to react before bailing out, he'll check his handhold to make sure he can unwrap the tail of the bull rope from his wrist. He might have time to unwrap it in one quick move while still riding with some degree of control. But if his hand is caught in the bull rope when he's headed for the ground, which is every rider's nightmare, it means big trouble; he'll be at the mercy of a ton of flesh—with horns. His only hope is to not panic, to work on the rope while staying upright, and to get quick aid from the bullfighters.

Kagan Sirett is a student at MSU in Bozeman. Like his counterpart, fellow Canadian Rob Bell, Kagan makes time for education in-between rodeos. Both of these young bull riders are already champions, and both have seriously injured their hands. They have also suffered from pulled muscles, concussions, and knee injuries, yet they were able to compete in the 2002 Olympic Command Performance Rodeo. About dismounting, Kagan explains: "When the whistle blows, I know I have to ride through and wait for a good time to get off. I know there is never a shortage of tests, but the best feeling in the world is getting through a situation where you're scared. The adrenaline makes me feel alive. Plus, I know that the bullfighters will do their best to help me out if I need it. They can bring out the best in a bull, but will also put their lives on the line to help."

KAGAN SIRETT FROM NEILBURG, SASKATCHEWAN, FACES A CHALLENGING EIGHT SECONDS ON THIS
SPOTTED BULL. EVEN THOUGH THE BULL HAS THROWN HIM IN THE AIR WITH A DRAMATIC MOVE,
KAGAN KEPT HIS BALANCE AND MANAGED TO PULL HIMSELF BACK DOWN ONTO THE BULL AND FINISH
OUT THE RIDE.

THOUGH KAGAN SIRETT MADE THE WHISTLE, HE WAS EN ROUTE TO BREAKING HIS RIDING HAND.

Bulls

Bulls come in a variety of sizes, crosses, and dispositions. The good ones get smarter after having bucked in a few rodeos and can be expected to develop a sizeable bag of tricks. Big bulls tend to be stronger than the smaller ones, but not as quick. They use their strength to jerk a rider forward over their horns each time they kick high and drop down in front, and they can build incredible momentum when they spin. Smaller bulls are usually much faster and can unseat their rider with lightning quick movements. No matter what their size, the toughest bulls to ride constantly change rhythm and direction. They might drift across the arena or jump forward after each kick. They might spin fast in a tight circle or rear up high in the front and then drop down low in order to direct all of their power to the rear end. These bulls never give up until the rider is gone.

In a Professional Bull Riders (PBR) event held in the early nineties, Tuff Hedeman scored a ninety-five on the famous bull Bodacious. It was a ride which, judges said later, they wished they'd scored higher, but Hedeman had the ride of his life. Bo was ridden successfully less than ten times in his career, by such notable cowboys as Bubba Dunn, Terry Don West, Greg Schlosser, Clint Branger, and Legs Stevenson. But because this great bull was directly responsible for putting too many cowboys in the hospital, his owner retired him from rodeo in 1995. He was inducted into the ProRodeo Hall of Fame in 1999 and grew to be a nationwide celebrity. Bodacious, or "The Yellow Whale," died in 2000 on the Andrews's ranch in Texas.

Judges

As in bareback and saddle bronc riding, two judges mark their score cards from inside the arena, with a third judge often timing and observing the run from behind the chutes. Bull and rider are separately awarded up to twenty-five points from each judge, and a combined score

When a bullfighter knows something about the bull ahead of time, he can anticipate its moves and often step in to help a cowboy get a better ride. Here, the bull had come out of the chute in a spin that was too close to the fence, and the bullfighter was able to change its behavior enough to allow the rider to put his talents on display.

in the eighties will be fairly common for a cowboy who manages to stay aboard for the required eight seconds.

The only time a perfect 100 has ever been given was in 1991 at the Wild Rogue Rodeo in Oregon, when Wade Leslie rode Growney Brothers' "Wolfman." A cowboy named Hall said about Wolfman: "Dynamite comes in small packages. If you can last eight seconds on this bull, he turns into a cash register." Wolfman was a grandson of Red Rock, a bull that remained unridden until he was brought out of retirement in 1988 for a series of special contests against World Champion Lane Frost, who rode him four out of seven times.

A contestant who not only maintains control of his ride, but who also shows he is willing to take extra risks by spurring, will receive a higher score than a rider who simply makes the eight-second whistle. As for scoring a bull, higher marks are awarded to an animal that tries hard, is extremely tough to ride, and uses every possible move to toss its rider.

PUTTING A HAND ON THE BULL'S HEAD WAS THE BEST POSSIBLE MOVE IN THIS SITUATION, WHERE A FALLEN RIDER IS AN OBVIOUS TARGET.

Bullfighters

When a bullfighter is of high enough caliber to work in professional rodeo, he usually knows the behavior patterns of most of the bulls and riders. What he doesn't know, he will learn prior to the event. With his knowledge and expertise, he can evoke slight changes in a bull's movement that go unnoticed by the audience, yet will immensely aid the rider. If, for example, a certain cowboy makes his strongest ride on a bull that spins to the right, and he draws a bull that consistently spins left, the bullfighter can often distract it just enough to change its direction. Or, if a bull has a reputation for throwing every rider the moment it bursts out of the chute, the bullfighter will know to stay close to the gate so he can distract it early, hoping either to change its pattern or be in position to defend a fallen rider.

Both bullfighters move into high gear when a rider gets his hand caught in the bull rope, and their combined actions are unbelievably quick and calculating. One will try to slow the animal down or divert its attention by putting himself directly in front of the bull's sight, while the other goes for the rope. Rodeo fans are lucky to be able to witness the abilities of these specialists who are out there in the arena, willing and able to put their lives on the line to assist.

Canadian rider Rob Bell was leading the world standings when he hurt his knee while trying to get off a bull. He had nothing but praise for the bullfighters who were there to help him. "I remember feeling my knee pop. It was just when I was getting thrown sideways. When I hit the ground I couldn't move; and those guys sure did a great job helping me."

Timed Events

A TIMED EVENT HORSE
ANTICIPATES THE JOB AHEAD
WITH TOTAL CONCENTRATION.
THIS HORSE HAS A BEAUTIFUL
HEADSTALL AND MATCHING
REINS, APROPOS TO HIS
STATUS.

Equipment and Terms for the Timed Events

ADDED MONEY: Financial compensation that is added to the contestant's entry fees and sponsor contributions that make up the total purse in an event.

BARRIER ROPE: A rope pulled across the front of the "box" where horse and rider wait. This barrier must stay in place until the calf or steer trips it by running into the arena.

BAT: A riding crop that is used on certain barrel or hazing horses to make them run faster. Some horses work harder just knowing their rider is holding a bat.

BELL BOOTS: Short rubber boots that fasten around the horse's front feet. These boots are used to protect a horse that has a tendency to hit its front feet with the back ones.

BITS AND HACKAMORES: Horses good enough to work at the professional level are well-trained and know their job, wearing bits or hackamores that are relatively gentle on the mouth or nose. Which one a rider chooses depends upon the horse's sensitivity. The most popular bits are those with a hinged mouthpiece, curbed ones with a high or low "port" in the middle, or hackamores with a shank to leverage control over the horse.

CLOTHING: Pro Rodeo dress standards call for every contestant to wear a cowboy hat, long-sleeved shirt with a collar, jeans, and boots. Certain sponsors help most of the cowboys, at least the ones who have qualified for the NFR, by paying them to wear their logos, brand of clothing, or use their equipment. Patches on shirt pockets and sponsor's names sewn along one of the sleeves are the only visible signs of sponsorship for timed-event contestants. Just as with the roughstock riders, however, sponsor benefits do not approach what other professional athletes earn.

CROSS FIRE: In team roping, if the heeler throws his rope before the header has changed a steer's direction, the team will be disqualified for a "cross fire."

LEG PROTECTION IS IMPORTANT FOR THE HORSES.

DALLY: (*dale vuelta* in Spanish, meaning "give it a turn") A technique used by ropers to control a steer that has been roped. The cowboy wraps, or dallies, his rope around the saddle horn to add strength to his hold on the rope. A team roper can adjust his dally by tightening up or by loosening his rope.

DAYLIGHTING: When a calf roper reaches his calf, it must be standing before it can be turned over and tied. If it is on the ground, the roper must first pick it up high enough that a judge can see daylight between its hooves and the ground.

DOG-FALL: When a steer is wrestled to the ground, its head and feet must be facing in the same direction or the throw is not considered legal. When this happens, the cowboy must reposition its head or let it get up so he can try again.

FLAGMAN: A rodeo official who uses a flag to signal the timers when to stop the clock.

GLOVES: Calf and team ropers now wear a simple white cotton glove on their roping hand. Leather gloves were popular up until three-time World Champion Team Roper Allen Bach found he could "feel" the rope better with a thinner and more pliable glove.

HARD AND FAST: Tying one end of the rope to the saddle horn. A team-roping heeler who is over the age of fifty may tie his rope hard and fast instead of being required to dally it around the horn.

HONDA: The eye in one end of a cowboy's lariat. The other end passes through the honda to form the loop.

HOOEY: A half-hitch knot made by a calf roper after he has made one or two wraps around three legs with his piggin' string.

HORN WRAPS: Padded protection worn by steers used in team roping to protect the base of their horns from rope burns.

HOULIHAN: A steer that tumbles head over heels when the bulldogger catches it.

LEG WRAPS OR POLO WRAPS: A rider protects the lower legs of his horse by wrapping them with soft, stretchy material that resembles a very wide Ace bandage.

MONEY BARREL: The first turn in barrel racing is the move that sets up the rest of a ride.

NO TIME: A cowboy who fails to qualify in a timed event receives a "no time" score from the flag judge, who signals his decision by waving his flag from side to side.

PANTY-HOSE: A team-roping term for what happens when a heeler's rope moves up above the hock toward the steer's flank.

A TOP ROPING HORSE IS WORTH EVERYTHING TO A COWBOY. IT DOES ITS JOB, DAY IN AND DAY OUT.

PEGGING: A steer is pegged when a bulldogger pushes the steer's horn into the ground.

PIGGIN' STRING: The smaller third rope used in calf roping; a quarter-inch round, three-ply nylon piece of rope six feet long. It is used to tie three of the calf's legs together to keep it from standing up and running away.

POWDER: Ropers often sprinkle baby powder in their rope bags to help take the moisture out of their ropes.

RATING OR RATE: Horse and rider learn to sense the speed and direction of cattle they work in their particular event. The ability to rate a cow is key to how well they will do in competition.

REIN: Ropers and steer wrestlers use a roping rein that is eight feet long and attaches to the bit or hackamore. The rein is in one piece so that it will stay around a horse's neck

ALTHOUGH CONCENTRATING ON BUSINESS, THE HAZING HORSE KNOWS HIS RIDER IS HOLDING A BAT. BOTH ARE WAITING FOR THE DOGGER TO NOD. THE HEADSTALL, BIT, REIN, AND TIE-DOWN ARE FAIRLY TYPICAL FOR THESE HORSES.

without the rider having to keep control of two single reins. Barrel racers use the same type of rein, but will often make a knot on either side of the middle to mark where they want to hold when cueing a horse to turn around a barrel.

RIM SHOES: Timed event horses need shoes that are grooved to provide stability and help them grab the ground.

ROPE: (*la reata* in Spanish, meaning "the rope") A cowboy's lariat, riata, lass-rope, or rope, is used as a lasso to rope an animal. Ropes dating back to the 1800s were originally made with plant fibers or braided horsehair. Rawhide came later, and then hemp. Today, lariats are made of grass hemp, or of nylon or poly/nylon blends that are durable and more resistant to temperature changes. The rope is considered to be an extension of a cowboy's arm. He chooses a particular length, weight, and flex to suit his needs, looking for a rope that is alive and has good balance. Once he has his favorites, he will take great care to protect them, because different weather conditions can affect the way a rope handles.

✳ Team roping headers use a fairly soft nylon/poly rope measuring thirty to thirty-two feet. Even though he may only need twenty feet of his rope to catch a steer, the extra length is there if he needs it. Also, he can use some of the extra length to let the rope slide around the horn when he dallies. This type of rope has more "life" and will fold around a steer's horns.

✳ Team roping heelers who rope the steer's hind legs use a slightly stiffer thirty-five-foot rope that holds its shape when the loop is thrown.

SADDLE: Generally, timed-event saddles are made of a wooden "tree" that is covered with rawhide and lined with sheepskin to protect the horse's back. Good saddles are designed to fit the horse, the rider, and the rider's particular needs.

✳ Roping saddles are sturdy, and the saddle horn (unless it belongs to a team-roping header) is wrapped with a piece of rubber so that the rope doesn't slip when he makes his dally. Seats are larger and longer than a bronc saddle, with narrow swells in front and a low cantle in the back. Stirrups support the rider's weight so he can stand up and lean forward to make his throw. The stirrups are wrapped with rawhide so that a boot can easily move in and out without getting stuck.

✳ Steer wrestling saddles have pear-shaped horns, lower cantles, slick seats, and wider stirrups to support the full weight of the rider. A neoprene girth is popular because it helps prevent the saddle from slipping when the cowboy transfers his weight onto the steer.

✳ Barrel saddles are light and form-fitting, with at least a four-inch cantle. The aluminum stirrups have a rawhide or rubber bottom that helps prevent slipping. Cinches are usually made of mohair string that does not bind the horse in any way. The best saddle pads are at least ¾-of-an-inch thick, fitted to both the horse and saddle, and made of wool.

SCORE: The distance between the front of the timed-event box and the scoreline in the arena. The length of a score depends upon the size of the box (from where the rider begins his run) and the length of the arena. A score is generally sixteen feet in front of the calf and team-roping box, and 12½ feet in front of a steer wrestling box.

✳ Roping and bulldogging. Since the barrier rope will not release until the calf or steer reaches the scoreline and trips the barrier, riders (and horses) learn to carefully anticipate the score. The timing of their start can add or subtract fractions of seconds to their run and make the difference between winning and losing.

SCORELINE: A predetermined line in the arena, measured according to the rules, that gives timed-event cattle a head start. A rider cannot pursue a calf or steer until it has reached this line. For example, the team-roping scoreline is set further out in the arena than a steer-wrestling line, so that the steer can run farther before the ropers are allowed to take off after it.

✶ Barrel racing. The scoreline for barrel racers marks the beginning and end of a run. The line placement is determined by the first five barrel racers to compete, in accordance with WPRA guidelines for different arena sizes. In pro rodeo, the line is always marked by an electric eye that is set up at the side. A judge stands behind this device, using his stopwatch as a backup in case of a malfunction.

SKID BOOTS: Padded protection for a horse's back legs. A horse that skids to a stop uses its back legs as brakes. Skid boots protect the fetlocks from being scraped on the ground.

SLACK: Competition that takes place before or after the main performances in rodeos that have a high number of contestants. Slack is open to the public and a quieter atmosphere for the cowboys and their horses.

SPLINT BOOTS: Leg protection for a horse's legs and tendons that help to buffer the extreme changes in momentum that occur during each ride.

SPURS: Just as in the roughstock events, spurs are designed specifically for each event and a cowboy's particular style. Most are made of steel or stainless steel, but the best and toughest ones are handcrafted from tempered steel. The rowels are dull so as not to hurt an animal's hide, and all spurs used in pro rodeo conform to strict regulation guidelines. It takes a good deal of practice to learn when and how to use a spur.

SPUR SHANK: A piece of metal that connects the spur to the rowel. Shanks vary in length, curve, and slant, depending on the size of a cowboy and his preference. Most timed-event riders use a short shank so they don't get caught up when trying to dismount and catch a calf or turn a steer.

TIE-DOWN: A strip of leather that clips onto the front of the cinch, between a horse's front legs, and connect to a band around its nose.

SADDLED UP AND READY FOR COMPETITION.

❄ Roping tie downs help prevent a horse from excitedly throwing its head up while in the start box anticipating the run. Tie-downs also help the horse to look straight ahead when turning and stopping.

❄ Barrel racing tie downs are useful for a horse that holds its head too high when entering and leaving the arena. They also help the horse maintain balance and control during the turns.

TIMERS: Every event has two official timers who work from the announcer's stand to start and stop the clock for each contestant. By their mutual agreement, a final time becomes official.

TRY: A horse that is exceptional in its will to do the job is referred to as having a lot of try.

TURFING: A term used by steer wrestlers that means wrestling a steer to the ground.

Steer Wrestling

N AFRICAN-AMERICAN/CHOCTAW rodeo star, named Will Pickett invented what cowboys call "bulldogging" in 1903. According to legend, he was having trouble separating a longhorn steer from the herd and finally jumped onto its back, taking it down by biting its lower lip like a bulldog as he turned the horns. The bulldog nickname stuck, and the contest grew from there. Steer wrestling is now the official name, and it is the fastest event in rodeo. The object is to catch a running steer from horseback and throw it down faster than anyone else. "Turfing" a steer in four or five seconds will most likely earn a paycheck, no matter what the size of the arena.

The steer is released from a chute that is usually situated between the steer wrestler and his partner, or "hazer." They can go after the steer once it reaches a predetermined line in the arena and trips a rope barrier stretched across the starting box. The two riders catch up quickly and sandwich the running steer between them. The steer wrestler must leave the saddle, catch the horns, and perform a half nelson on the steer to bring it to the ground. Time stops when the steer is on its side with its feet and head pointing in the same direction.

A perfect combination of factors is required to produce a winning time. The arena footing must be deep enough for a rider to dig his heels into when he has caught his steer; the steer needs to run straight and not too fast; the dogger, his hazing partner, and both horses must react at the right moments as a team.

Cowboys participating in this event are often called "the linebackers of rodeo."

Tom Camarillo slides over to his steer.

SLACK ON A PERFECT SUMMER MORNING REPRESENTS THE VERY BEST OF RODEO. THE HORSES ARE WELL CARED FOR, THE COWBOYS DRESSED WITH PRIDE, AND THE EVENT FILLED WITH HISTORY.

Preparation

A competitive steer wrestler has to have a lot of practice "rating" steers on horseback, catching, and turfing them. He must also have one or two very good horses, a hazing partner, and a willingness to spend time traveling to many rodeos. Most of these cowboys have grown up around horses and cattle and are big enough to wrestle a 600-pound steer to the ground. By the time they hit the rodeo circuit, they have learned a technique that suits them, studied ways to improve, and are in excellent physical condition.

Most bulldoggers know each other from many small rodeos and local practices, and have found various hazers around the country that they can work with. Some team up for several months, either traveling together or meeting up at the rodeos; others know a few men they can count on to be at the same rodeos. Either way, a smart steer wrestler pairs up with the very best hazer he can find—even if the hazer happens to be a fellow bulldogger competing against him in the same rodeo.

Trained and seasoned horses are a commodity, and these cowboys rarely have more than one or two they can really count on. Steer wrestlers and hazers spend a lot of time looking for just the right horse, often choosing to "finish" ones that have had prior training. If there's room in the trailer, a less experienced horse may be included in many road trips to give it exposure to rodeo life.

> *Bulldogger and hazer Rod Lyman takes great pride in finding a young horse that is somewhat familiar with cattle and roping, then training it to become a top heading or hazing horse. "I love the training part," he says. "It's rewarding to figure out a horse and bring him along. It takes years to get one to the point where he is really solid. Horses are under a lot of pressure these days, and they can be ruined if they go to a lot of rodeos before they're ready." Rod and his wife, Stefani, are on the road an average of 250 days a year. They take along their dogs, her barrel horse, and four horses that are in different stages of training. Rod is highly respected in the world of rodeo for his accomplishments, good attitude, and willingness to share his knowledge with others. Most importantly, he is someone who truly loves what he is doing.*

Unlike roughstock contestants who learn their draws in advance and then decide which rodeos to attend, a steer wrestler only learns his draw an hour before the rodeo begins. He therefore has to make an early commitment to the rodeos he enters because his normal mode of transportation is by road; and at least one or two of his traveling partners are prized horses. Given those considerations, a bulldogger who is trying to make this sport his livelihood will expect to put about 125,000 miles a year on truck and trailer.

Arrival and Warming Up

The first thing a timed-event cowboy does when he arrives is take care of his horse, or horses if he is fortunate enough to have more than one. Like people, horses need time to settle down and get used to their new surroundings before they can be expected to work. Some doggers arrive without a horse, choosing to borrow from another contestant while their own horse stays home to rest up. But the

THE TIMED-EVENT BOSS MAKES SURE THAT THE BARRIER ROPE IS PROPERLY SET. WHEN HE IS SATISFIED ALL IS READY, THE STOCK CONTRACTOR WILL PUT HIS HAND ON THE RED LEVER AT THE TOP OF THE CHUTE AND WAIT FOR THE DOGGER TO NOD.

Joey Bell and his horse are ready to go, but he is waiting for the "pusher" to get the steer standing evenly on both back legs.

agreement to borrow a horse means splitting any prize money with the owner. Communication is good among cowboys; they all know who will be at the rodeo, who needs a hazing partner, and who is home nursing a sore back or bruised ribs.

At a big rodeo, slack is always the first round of competition, and it begins early in the morning. Open to the public, it's an excellent time to watch many contestants in each event who are vying for prize money. The bulldoggers learn their draw, prepare their horses and warm them up in the arena. Then, although they seem to be fairly casual while standing around and visiting during the event, these men always have their eyes on the steers. Each steer has its own way of coming out of the start gate and running, and it tends to act the same way every time. Even though a cowboy might draw a steer that isn't very good, there is definitely an advantage to being able to anticipate the upcoming run and make a game plan.

WITH THE FOCUS OF A CHAMPION, ROD LYMAN WAITS FOR THE RIGHT MOMENT TO MAKE HIS NOD. A SLIGHT TIP OF HIS HAT SIGNALS THE STOCK CONTRACTOR TO TRIP THE GATE MECHANISM.

Whether competing in slack or during a rodeo performance, horses need to be loosened up and ready. Ideally, the warm-up process takes place in the arena itself, or a nearby field or race track where the horse can trot and lope. Indoor rodeos present more of a problem. With only asphalt outside, the space for preparing horses is at one small end of the arena—so small, in fact, that walking in circles is the only way to prepare.

Just before the event begins, the riders check their equipment and make sure everything is ready and secure. Saddles are snugged, bridles and tie-downs checked, legs wrapped, and splint and bell boots are put on. Judges in the arena also make ready. They determine where the scoreline will be and mark it by laying a piece of rope in the dirt. This line is generally about four feet in front of the chute, but the exact line depends upon the length of the arena and the depth of the rider's start box. Then they measure out a length of rope that will be looped around each steer just before it starts. The other end of that rope is connected to a spring-loaded mechanism on the gate. This mechanism keeps the barrier rope in place across the front of the rider's box. When the steer runs forward and crosses the score, it pulls the rope and trips the mechanism holding the barrier rope taut. The moment the red flag on the rope moves, the timers start their clocks running.

Helpers organize the steers according to the draws. This activity, though unseen by the audience, must run smoothly—a lot of entry fees and prize money depend upon how calmly the cattle are handled. One of the helpers climbs down behind the front steer and waits for the event to begin. His job is to make sure the steer is ready and to push him forward when the gate opens. Often, the stock contractor controls the gate release. He stands next to the gate with his hand on the trigger, waiting for the cowboy's nod to open the chute.

Last to move into place are the contestants, who walk their horses into the timed-event boxes on either side of the chute. In some rodeos, the two riders must begin from the same box, which adds difficulty. But the contestants and their horses all know what to expect. They are used to the routine: settle down, get positioned correctly, and concentrate on business. The bulldogger takes a quick look at his hazer, the steer, and the judges. He makes sure his horse is backed up in the corner of the box, standing evenly on all fours, and looking ahead. His nod starts the run.

Many sets of brothers compete as professionals in rodeo. Todd and Randy Suhn have certainly made names for themselves as top steer wrestlers. Both have qualified several times for the National Finals Rodeo. Todd is from Colorado, and Randy lives in Wyoming.

RANDY SUHN DEMONSTRATES HIS INTENSE FOCUS AND GREAT ABILITY. HE HAS A HARD RUNNING STEER, IN A MUDDY ARENA, BUT HE CAN MAKE AN EASY TRANSFER BECAUSE HIS HORSE IS DOING A PERFECT JOB.

The Run

THE STEER WRESTLER. When the chute opens, the steer must get to the scoreline and trip the barrier rope before the rider starts, or ten seconds will be added to the final time. The dogger and his horse both know they have to

CASH MEYERS LEAVES THE BOX A MILLISECOND AFTER HIS STEER REACHES THE SCORELINE, HITTING THE BARRIER ROPE THE INSTANT IT STARTS TO FALL.

wait for that rope to trip loose, but the timing of their start is crucial to the win. A split-second later, they are off. The steer wrestler closes in from the steer's left at a dead run. When he senses the time is right, he leans over, placing all of his weight on the right stirrup as he reaches for the steer's horns. Depending upon his style, he might reach for the left, inside horn with his left hand. This way, he can use his body weight to push down on the horn and tilt the steer's head. The more traditional method is to go for the right horn, because he can hook his right arm underneath it, using strength and leverage to turn the steer's head and slow it down.

He leaves his horse even before he has hold of the horns, and uses the horse's momentum to carry his feet ahead of the steer so he can drop them into the dirt—just like a broad jumper. Using his legs and heels as brakes, the dogger twists the steer's head away from him and pulls the horns toward his chest. He grabs the nose to get more leverage, and waits for the right moment to upset its balance. A quick hip check against the front shoulder should bring the steer down. But it isn't always that easy. Sometimes a steer will suddenly slow down, just

as the rider has reached the point of no return between horse and steer. At speeds of twenty-five or thirty miles per hour, the rider may find himself augured into the dirt. Other times, because steers are so elastic, the rider can turn its nose to the sky only to have the steer dog-fall in the opposite direction.

THE HAZER. The first move a hazer makes must be fast and accurate if he is to help the steer run in a straight line down the arena. Sometimes he knows the animal from prior events and can prepare accordingly. For instance, if the steer tends to dodge to the right when it starts, the hazer will know he has to bolt from the gate in order to alter this pattern. Other times, especially early in the season when steers are new and their habits unfamiliar, he and his horse must concentrate solely on where and how the steer is running. With one eye on the steer and one on the dogger, the hazer then rates the steer's course until the bulldogger has gotten hold of the horns and is in a good position. Then he moves closer, helping to turn the steer and slow its momentum. This is a tricky maneuver. The hazer needs to stay near enough to turn the steer, but not so close as to step on the dogger's legs when they're jammed into the dirt ahead of him. The hazer has to watch and anticipate—his horse has to react instantly to leg pressure.

After the steer is down and the judge has dropped his flag to signal time, the hazer will catch his partner's horse and bring it back to the starting point. Often, a hazer leaves the arena only to turn around and help the next cowboy.

This cowboy shows his athleticism and balance as he moves onto the back of his steer. He leaves his foot in the stirrup, letting the horse's momentum carry his leg forward so he can plant both feet in the dirt ahead of him. This critical changeover has been the cause of many accidents in the past (if a rider's foot gets caught, he can be dragged or trampled), but with today's experienced horses and riders, the injury rate is considerably lower.

Horses

Most steer-wrestling and hazing horses are either a mix of Thoroughbred and Quarter Horse, or just pure Quarter Horse, because of build and temperament. Riders use a more compact animal today, because modern arenas tend to be smaller and everything happens in shorter bursts of speed. The basic requirements are good conformation, a strong back, speed, and a good mind. After that, years of experience and maturity are imperative to their development. In fact, a "young" horse in this event would be considered as coming into its prime at the age of thirteen, where many of the top horses are approaching twenty.

Ivan Teigen, a Montana cattle and sheep rancher who has won over half a million dollars has a straightforward view of his sport: "Even if it's been said a lot of times, it is still true. You're only as good as your horse."

MONTANA NATIVE JUSTIN DAVIS COMES FROM A LONG LINE OF FAMILY INVOLVED IN THE CATTLE AND RANCHING BUSINESS. IN PERFECT FORM, HE HAS HOOKED HIS RIGHT ARM UNDER THE STEER'S HORN AND IS USING HIS OTHER ARM AND HIP TO APPLY ENOUGH PRESSURE TO TURN IT ON ITS SIDE.

A **DOGGING HORSE** has to have timing. A good one senses the exact moment to start after a steer, which is critical for an event that is decided in milliseconds. Then it has to run flat out, track the steer, and put its rider in position to dismount. After the rider leaves its back, this horse is expected to keep running straight until well past the steer—not something easily taught.

A good **HAZING HORSE** is worth its weight in gold. Often slightly smaller in build, it has to run just as fast, if not faster, than a dogging horse, and be able to rate a steer. Cowboys say that an agile and quick-footed hazing horse that has cow sense, yet still takes direction from its rider, will help a good bulldogging horse last much longer.

Many of these horses are so good at their job, and so well-seasoned, that other competitors and hazers want to use them. Lending a horse to a few

THIS GREAT TEAM COMBINES SOUTH DAKOTA AND MONTANA. BIRCH NEGAARD IS STARTING TO SHIFT HIS WEIGHT TOWARD THE STEER WHILE ROD LYMAN CLOSES IN. BOTH HORSES ARE RESPONDING CORRECTLY, AND BIRCH'S HORSE HAS EVEN CHANGED LEADS TO SUPPORT A MOVE TO THE LEFT.

other cowboys has long been common procedure in steer wrestling, but the stakes are higher these days, and most owners don't want to overuse their good horses or expose them to someone whose horsemanship skills are not up to par—a horse at the pro level has learned to trust its rider; bad handling can easily negate that trust. When a heading horse is loaned to another rider, and the owner hazes for him, the unspoken agreement is that the owner will receive 25 percent of the winnings. If a hazing horse is loaned out to someone helping another bulldogger, the owner receives 12.5 percent of any profits.

Steers

Weighing between 450 and 750 pounds to qualify for an approved bulldogging event, the best steers are three- or four-year-old Mexican Corrientes with well-developed, flat horns that measure about 1½ to 2 feet. As the name implies, Corriente cattle originated in Mexico and many are still shipped from there through El Paso to stock contractors, steer wrestlers, and team ropers all over the United States and Canada. The breed is known for being docile, long lasting, and quite sturdy. But these steers are also very smart. If treated well, and used only a

few times a day over the course of the rodeo, they improve over the year. If worked too hard, they will do just about anything to avoid being caught and turfed. A steer that changes momentum or direction or ducks its head will most likely cause problems for a bulldogger and his partner.

A DOGGING HORSE IS TRAINED TO CONTINUE RUNNING STRAIGHT AHEAD AFTER ITS RIDER HAS LEFT THE SADDLE. THIS STEER CHANGED DIRECTION AFTER ROD LYMAN CAUGHT IT, TAKING PRECIOUS SECONDS OFF THE CLOCK. NEITHER THE HAZER NOR HIS HORSE COULD DO MORE TO HELP.

T.W. Parker digs into the dirt to slow the steer down and turn it. Bulldogging is not without its injuries, and T. W. has had his share of shoulder and knee problems.

Just as other timedevent cattle, bulldogging steers must be numbered for identification, with permanent brands on the left horn or left side.

Judges

There are two judges for this event. One stands to the left of the steer wrestler's box so he can watch the start and determine whether it is legal. He makes sure the steer, not the horse, trips the barrier rope, and drops his flag to start the clock running. The other judge is on a horse halfway down the arena. Both watch for the bulldogger to make his catch and turf the steer correctly. If the steer isn't brought to a stop, or is turned before hitting the ground, the dogger is disqualified. The judge on horseback drops his flag, stopping the clock when the steer falls on its side, with its legs and head pointing in the same direction.

SOME STEERS ARE SO ELASTIC THAT THEY DO NOT HAVE TO GIVE IN EASILY. THE DOGGER IS
DOING EVERYTHING HE CAN TO MAKE IT FALL, WHILE THE FLAG JUDGE STANDS READY, AND
PRECIOUS SECONDS TICK AWAY.

Team Roping

TEAM ROPING IS RODEO'S ONLY true team event, as both contestants can earn prize money. It requires a successful combination of skills from two riders and their horses to rope and immobilize a steer. This event began as ranch work, where catching a steer for doctoring or re-branding was too much of a job for one cowboy. If the cowboys could rope a steer around the horns and back feet simultaneously, each could keep their ropes taut, immobilizing the steer between them while a third person could safely work on the animal. This technique is still used on ranches today when chutes are not available; it has also become a big part of professional rodeo.

In this event, the steer is given a slight head start from a chute at one end of the arena. Standing to either side of that chute, two ropers on horseback must wait behind a rope barrier until the steer trips a mechanism that releases it. When the barrier drops, the cowboys give chase. Although the two contestants begin their run almost simultaneously, the header ropes first. After he has settled his lasso over the steer's horns or neck, the heeler throws out his loop, catching the steer's rear feet. Timing stops when both cowboys and their horses are facing each other and the steer is caught between them.

A successful team consists of two highly skilled riders (women also compete in this event) who work well together, combining different skills. But their success is also determined by the steer that is "drawn" and by having exceptional horses. By posting times under about five

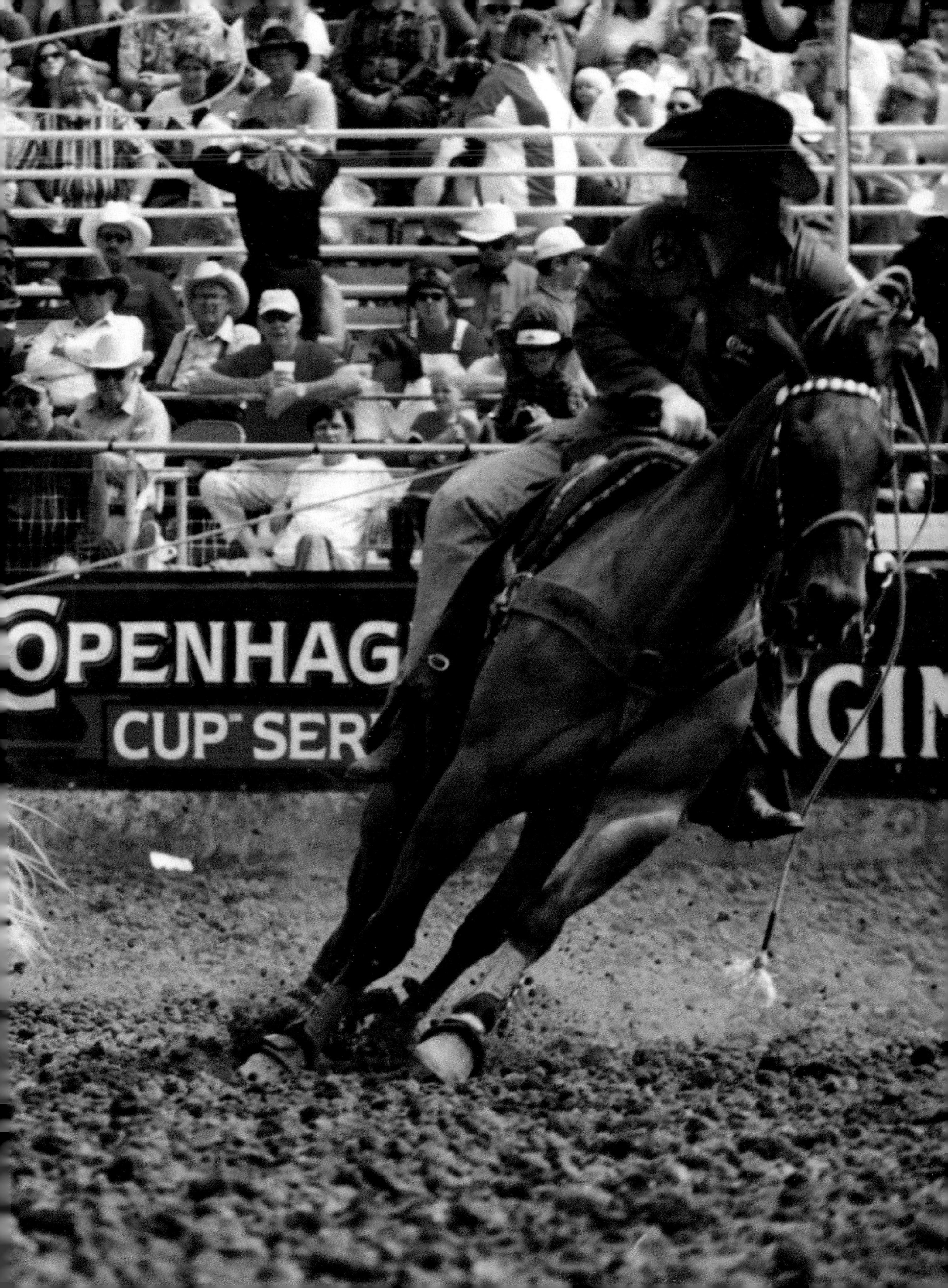
OPENHAG
CUP SER
GIN

seconds, "header" and "heeler" can each expect to earn upwards of $100,000 a year at the high end of competition.

Groundwork and Planning

Becoming proficient takes years and years of practice. Almost every professional roper today will say that he grew up with a rope in his hands—the family pet being his first moving target. He then spent many years learning to be a good horseman. After mastering these two skills, the roper might go to teaching clinics around the country to learn more about heading or heeling techniques. Eventually he will choose the specialty that suits him and develop his technique over long hours in the practice pen, roping sometimes as many as 100 steers a day. During this time, he will also be searching for the right partner to complement his skills—and for a horse or two that can carry him to success.

When ropers team up together, they face a series of logistical nightmares. They have to agree on which rodeos to go to, and must coordinate travel arrangements, making sure that their three or four horses stay in top condition while on the road. Often a team will enter two or three rodeos scheduled for the same weekend. If the first rodeo "go-round" happens to be on Wednesday morning, they have enough time to pack up and drive to another rodeo the same afternoon or evening. Team ropers range from ages eighteen to over fifty, and many of them choose to spend a good part of the year driving all over the U.S. and Canada, making their living, and living their lives, in rodeo.

Arrival and Preparation

These cowboys often have little time to spare between rodeos and will arrive with just enough time to unload and saddle up. They usually congregate at the rodeo office to pay entry fees and find out their draw for the competition. Then they make a game plan. Some steers consistently run fast and straight down the arena while others will duck or swerve to avoid being roped. Knowing the steer and what to expect will aid the run.

Before the rodeo begins, helpers move the steers into pens at the end of the arena and fasten the protective horn wraps. They match each numbered steer with the contestant and then leave the animals alone to settle down. Handling the steers quietly and correctly during this process is critical, and the cowboys depend upon the rodeo personnel to ensure this

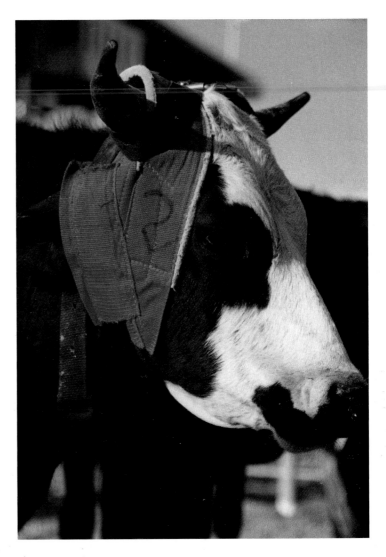

A STEER IN HORN WRAPS.

happens. The judges also have to prepare. They look over the start boxes and the chute, inspect the barrier equipment, and determine where the scoreline should be. Then they measure the distance from the front of the chute to that line. A thin rope of the same length is looped over the steer's head; the other end is attached to a mechanism that releases the rope barrier across the front of the header's box. The steer is released first, and when it reaches the scoreline, it breaks the rope and triggers the barrier-release mechanism. As soon as the barrier rope falls, the cowboys can go after their steer.

The ropers make sure their horses are warmed up. Trotting and loping can be pretty difficult at some rodeos, especially in a coliseum, where only a small area is set aside for this activity. But the action in timed events is intense, and a horse's muscles must be ready or legs can be injured. After warming up, each rider wraps his horse's legs, puts on skid boots, and adjusts the saddle and bridle. He also might warm up by doing some stretches, but soon he's

on his horse, focusing on the ride ahead and preparing his ropes. He chooses a rope he feels will be right for the weather conditions and type of cattle, and then may fill the waiting time with straightening, coiling, swinging, and then re-coiling the rope.

The Run

When team roping is about to begin, helpers move the steers in correct sequence through the chute. The judge loops the measured string rope over the horns of the front steer and attaches the other end to the mechanism controlling the gate release. A cattle pusher moves in close behind the steer to steady it and keep it facing straight ahead while the contestants ride into their start boxes. A judge pulls the barrier rope across the front, and each roper readies his horse, making sure it is well-positioned for the start, standing squarely, and concentrating. The header decides when it's time to let the steer go.

Each roper carries one rope and is only allowed to throw one loop (one to the front and one in back), unless the rodeo has more than two go-rounds, where a third loop (front or back) is allowed. The steer starts the clock running. When it reaches the predetermined scoreline and trips the barrier rope in front of the header's box, the flag attached to the rope moves, signaling the timers to start their watches. Both ropers are then

CLAY TRYAN WAITS IN THE START BOX FOR THE STEER TO
BE POSITIONED JUST RIGHT. HE HOLDS THE COILS AND
REIN IN HIS LEFT HAND, WHICH HE WILL LOWER AS SOON
AS HE IS READY TO RELEASE HIS HORSE. HIS GLOVED
RIGHT HAND IS POISED TO SWING AND OPEN THE LOOP
JUST AS SOON AS HE NODS FOR THE STEER TO BE
RELEASED. CONCENTRATION AND PATIENCE ARE WHAT
MAKE THIS YOUNG COWBOY SO SUCCESSFUL.

allowed to go after the steer. Although their start is almost concurrent, header and heeler have very different jobs to perform—and very different expectations of their horses.

THE HEADER has many responsibilities, and precise timing at the start is critical to the entire run. He has to anticipate how his horse will react that day, and know the size of his starting box, the length of the "score," and the type of steer he is working. When he's ready, he sets his horse in position, almost cocked against the back corner of the box and standing evenly on all four feet. At the same time, he checks on the readiness of his partner, the steer, the helper behind the steer, and the gate man. With both horses set up and ropes ready, his nod signals the chute to open. His release on the reins is critical. He wants the barrier rope to break away an instant before it is hit by his horse's chest. If he and his horse are able to get a jump on the steer, he might be able to intimidate it and position himself to control the entire run.

Ideally, the header catches the steer by curling his rope around both horns. He can also rope the neck, or the nose and one horn (called "half a head"), but his control over the way the steer moves will be compromised. If he misses his first throw, he can try again with a second loop. Once the "catch" is made, he takes up the slack in the rope and dallies it counterclockwise around his saddle horn. At the same moment, he moves his horse left, changing momentum and towing the steer along behind him. This is called "setting" the steer, and it has to be done correctly.

THE TEAM OF CLAY TRYAN AND CALEB TWISSELMAN RUN FLAT OUT, CHASING A FAST STEER ON MUDDY
GROUND.

CLAY HAS THROWN HIS LOOP AROUND THE HORNS AND WILL QUICKLY TIGHTEN IT WHILE HE SIGNALS
HIS HORSE TO TURN TO THE LEFT. WITH LOOP READY, CALEB WAITS FOR HIS CHANCE TO THROW.

THE WELL-KNOWN HEADER/HEELER TEAM, BOBBY HURLEY AND MIKE BEERS, OFTEN COMPETE TOGETHER AROUND THE COUNTRY. HERE, THEY ARE IN THE FIRST ROUND OF SLACK AT THE CODY STAMPEDE, ONE OF THE MANY STOPS DURING THE FOURTH OF JULY SERIES CALLED "COWBOY CHRISTMAS."

The header not only wants to slow the steer down, but also to pull it to the left and in a straight line, so that the heeler can come in behind with a good angle to rope its back legs. Should the header pull the steer sideways instead, it will swing its weight to the outside, creating a difficult angle for the other roper. When the heeler has made his catch, the header, with rope taut, turns his horse to face the steer.

Charles Pogue had a wonderful gray/white horse named Scooter. The two have a long history of championships, but they parted ways awhile ago when Scooter died of pneumonia. Charles is a family man and a churchgoer. He ropes often with his wife, who is also a header, and they now have a baby girl to bring into the world of roping. "I set my goals and then work my tail off to achieve them," he says. "But I've roped all my life. You really have to grow up with a rope in your hand or you can't compete nationally."

THE HEELER tries to come out of the box just a little behind the header. He starts by running straight or slightly to the left, coaxing, or "hazing," the steer to run at an angle. If his approach is too aggressive, he might force the steer to turn sharply, hurting the chances for his header

BOBBY HURLEY HAS MADE HIS DALLY AND IS IN THE PROCESS OF TURNING THE STEER SO HIS HEELER CAN LEGALLY ROPE THE BACK FEET. HIS HORSE HAS TO MAKE DRAMATIC CHANGES IN A SHORT PERIOD. FIRST HE GALLOPS STRAIGHT AHEAD, THEN HAS TO MAKE A SHARP LEFT TURN, THEN STOP, MAKE A 180-DEGREE-TURN, AND BACK UP TO TIGHTEN THE ROPE.

to rope quickly. Once the header has thrown his loop, the heeler quickly moves his horse sideways so that he can see the steer's back feet. This requires a sudden change of speed and a sharp move to the left—all while he is preparing to throw. In order to avoid disqualification for an infraction called "crossfire," the steer must be physically pulled a step in the header's direction before the heeler can rope its back legs.

The heeler now has the difficult job of trying to catch both rear feet instantaneously. He uses his rope to set a trap, laying the loop almost on the ground, and waits for the steer to step into it. The accuracy of his timing is critical, and so fast that most will be unable to see it. If he rushes and pulls the loop closed too quickly, he might catch only one leg and incur a five-second penalty. As his loop tightens around the feet or legs, he dallies his rope and pulls it taut, facing the steer.

Mike Beers won the world championships when he was twenty-four and has since qualified for the National Finals twenty times. Although his main event is team roping, this heeler is also known for his abilities in steer and calf roping. "I knew what I wanted to do at the age of seven. My dad was a hard-

TRAVIS TRYAN HAS MADE HIS CATCH AND TURNED HIS HORSE AND THE STEER TO THE LEFT. HE WATCHES FOR HIS HEELER, MATT ROBERTSON, TO PULL THE LOOP TIGHT BEFORE HE TURNS BACK TOWARD THE STEER. MATT WON THE RESISTOL OVERALL ROOKIE OF THE YEAR AWARD IN 2001.

TRAVIS TRYAN HAS TAKEN THE TEAM ROPING CIRCUIT BY STORM.
BOTH HE AND HIS BROTHER CLAY QUALIFIED FOR THE 2001
WRANGLER NATIONAL FINALS RODEO IN THEIR FIRST SERIOUS
YEAR OF PROFESSIONAL COMPETITION.

working restaurant owner whose greatest love was roping, and he supported me when I decided to follow my dream." Mike and Bonnie Beers host over twenty roping schools each year at their ranch in Oregon.

When time is official, each rider moves forward, shaking out their loops to free the steer. Once their work is done, roper and heeler walk back toward the exit, each busy re-coiling their ropes and quietly reviewing the run.

Horses

Ropers are the first to say that the right horse makes all the difference between winning and losing. These animals are trained to respond quickly to the way steers move and to how a rider rides. It takes time and expertise to develop a heading or heeling horse. They are not even introduced to cattle and roping until about four or five years old. It takes even longer before they are seasoned and mentally ready to perform with consistency. Good rope horses are considered to be in their prime between the ages of ten and seventeen.

HEADING HORSES are usually Quarter Horses or a mix of Quarter Horse and Thoroughbred. Measuring 15.1 to 15.2 hands, they tend to be slightly larger and more powerful than heeling horses, because they have to pull a steer along after it has been roped. These horses need to learn to run hard toward the left side of a steer, turn left when it has been roped, and stop.

They also must learn to be absolutely ready when they walk into the start box, standing squarely, cocked against the back corner, ready to explode as soon as the rider releases the reins. When the rope is thrown, they must move somewhat sideways to the left until told to turn, face the steer, and stand still. Good, consistent heading horses are prized possessions, known to all contestants, and are stars on the rodeo circuit for many years.

HEELING HORSES are often smaller than headers and are almost always full Quarter Horses. They are known to be "cowy," or to have built-in cow sense and anticipate what a steer is going to do next. These horses must be durable, ready to run at whatever speed their rider asks and to keep as far to the right of a steer as directed. Then they have to stay to the right of the steer

THIS STEER, THOUGH PANTY-HOSED BY THE HEELER'S ROPE, IS PROPERLY IMMOBILIZED BETWEEN HEADER AND HEELER.

TAMMY WEST CAN HOLD HER OWN AS A TEAM-ROPING HEADER ON THE CIRCUIT.

until told to go into slow motion, turning hard to the left in order to be on the other side of the steer so their rider can rope the hind legs. When asked to stop, heeling horses stand still until directed otherwise.

Just like headers, good heeling horses are extremely valuable. They are great athletes and will be treated as such throughout their career and into retirement.

Steers

The cattle used in team roping average about 500 pounds, but must weigh between 450 and 650 pounds in order to qualify for a PRCA-approved rodeo. They are numbered by an identifiable permanent brand located on their right side or right horn, and they must all wear horn wraps. The Mexican Corriente breed is used in competition, although Longhorns are often the choice for practice because they are less expensive. Corrientes are strong, extremely adaptive, and well-built. Their horns are heavier at the base than in other breeds and they only grow to a certain length.

Most of the steers roped during slack are used later in the rodeo performances. After being used in several rodeos, they learn where the "catch pen" is at the other end of the arena, and will naturally run toward it. Some experienced steers don't mind the routine and will run straight and not too fast every time—the type every cowboy hopes to draw. Others, however, become savvy and learn to avoid a rope. They might duck their heads, slow down, change direction, or try to stop and fight the rope. A tough, smart steer can throw off a cowboy's pace just enough to keep the team from earning any money.

Judges

Two judges stand to the left of the riders at the beginning of this run. In bigger rodeos, a third judge will be in place at the other end of the arena to help watch for penalties. The judge closest to the chute and header's box observes the start. If he sees the header (instead of the steer) break the barrier rope, a ten-second penalty is given. This judge then moves forward to watch the rest of the run from a better position. After making sure there is a legal head catch, the judges then watch to see if the header pulls the steer at least one full jump toward him before the heeler releases his rope. They will disqualify the team for "crossfire" if this does not happen. If the heeler throws his loop and catches only one back leg, five seconds are added to the final time. Finally, both riders must be facing each other, with the upright steer stretched out between them, before the flag judge stops the time. Should the steer be pulled too hard, a judge will impose a fine on the contestants and disqualify them.

Calf Roping

CALF ROPING WAS AROUND LONG BEFORE ITS DEBUT IN rodeo, and ranchers worldwide still use this age-old technique to brand or doctor a sick calf. It was, and is, the quickest way for one person to catch and immobilize an animal without the benefit of corrals or chutes. An extremely popular sport today, calf roping is not limited to the young. In fact, "ropings" occur somewhere in the United States and Canada almost every single day of the year. When a good calf roper decides to turn pro, he (or she) has a chance at earning over $200,000 a year.

Although the fundamentals of roping a calf remain the same, riding and roping styles have been honed and refined over the years by people like Dean Oliver, Toots Mansfield, Roy Cooper, and many others. Calf roping is said to be rodeo's most complex event because so many variables are involved. The goal is to rope a running calf from horseback and immobilize it in the shortest time possible. A professional can do this in less than nine seconds. The key variables are the weight of the calf and the length of the arena. Both horse and rider in this event each have very specific jobs that require speed, accuracy, and good instincts.

The rider has to be an excellent horseman and roper, able to pair his actions with those of his horse and the calf. He starts his pursuit at a dead run, after the calf has gotten a head start and reaches a specific line in the arena. Galloping at full speed and swinging his lasso overhead, he throws the rope at just the right moment and loops it around the calf's neck. He dismounts while his horse slides to a stop. Then he runs to the calf, catches and "flanks" it onto the ground. Gathering up any three legs, he ties them together with a "piggin' string" and throws both arms in the air signaling that he is done. Time stops, but the competition continues as the cowboy returns to his horse,

WORLD-CLASS BULLDOGGER AND CALF ROPER K.C. JONES MAKES HIS CATCH.

gets on, and walks him forward to slacken the rope. If the calf kicks loose before six seconds have elapsed, the rider receives a score of "no time."

POPLARVILLE, MISSISSIPPI, IS WHERE THIS YOUNG COWBOY WAS RAISED. MARCUS TRAVELS TO MANY RODEOS IN NORTH AMERICA WITH HIS DAD, WORLD CHAMPION HERBERT THERIOT.

A good roping horse will stand fairly still in the box until the calf has been released, then burst forward to track and "rate" the calf ahead of him. The moment the horse feels a pull on the bit, it knows to slide to a stop while the rider is in the process of dismounting. Then, without guidance from the rider, the horse will back up until it feels the rope is taut and stand still while the rider finishes tying his calf. Only when the rider gets back into his saddle will it move forward and release tension on the rope.

Training and preparation

Horse and rider are partners, as in all timed events. The rider knows how to rope, flank, and tie a calf, while the horse must be able to sprint, rate a calf, stop quickly, and stand still when the rope is taut.

Rope handling is an art that takes years to master. Most ropers learn at an early age how to hold, coil, swing, and throw a rope, and how to take up the slack after looping the rope around a stationary object. Later, after they've learned how to flank and tie a calf quickly and effectively, they combine roping with riding skills, learning how to rope from a horse and to dismount while moving. A calf roper needs to have plenty of experience—and a good horse—before competing in big rodeos. The ability of both horse and rider to perform well under pressure separates the winners from the losers. For this event, it's often said that winning in the big leagues comes from between the ears.

Arrival and Slack

Horse care comes first when a roper arrives at the rodeo grounds; weary from travel, everyone needs a day of rest. During this down time, the rodeo secretary makes the draws from a hat, pairing calf with roper and determining the sequence. Competition at the bigger rodeos begins in the morning, during slack. With few spectators or distractions, slack is a more relaxed time for the cowboys because they are allowed to be inside the arena with their horses, where they can visit and watch the cattle. If they win, they qualify for the finals. If they don't win, they have ample time to pack up their gear and head for the next rodeo.

Even though the arena conditions are the same, roping times during slack might be faster than in the afternoon or evening performances, due to the horses and riders standing

on either side of the chute. Their presence creates a pathway for the calves, causing them to run in a straighter line. During the "perfs" where noise and lights and nerves abound, confused calves sometimes run to the side instead of toward the exit.

Oklahoma's Blair Burk can hit five rodeos over the Fourth of July weekend. He learned about life on the road from his family. "I guess I can say that I grew up in the backseat going to rodeos. My father won the NFR average title in 1973." Now, Blair is carrying on the tradition by being a perennial contender for the lead in world standings.

Warm-up and Ready

Preparing the cattle for the roping event is generally the same as for steer wrestling and team roping. Numbered and sorted according to the draw, the animals are moved toward the chutes. Meanwhile, the calf ropers warm up their horses wherever they can find room to walk or trot, while judges measure and mark the scoreline and the length of the "breakaway" cord. As in steer wrestling and team roping, one

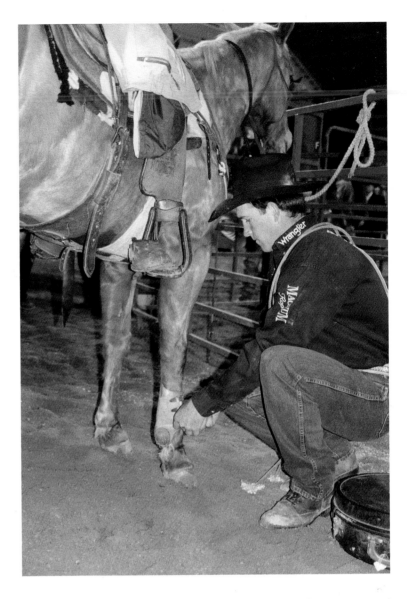

HAVING JUST FINISHED COMPETITION AT THE DODGE NATIONAL FINALS CIRCUIT IN POCATELLO, IDAHO, K.C. JONES ATTENDS TO HIS HORSE EVEN BEFORE PUTTING HIS ROPE AWAY. BRIDLE IS OFF, CINCH LOOSENED, BELL BOOTS AND SPLINT BOOTS HAVE BEEN REMOVED. AN ALL-AROUND HAND AND CHAMPION, K.C. CAN TAKE HIS MANY TALENTS WITH HIM WHEN HE TRAVELS THE CIRCUIT. NOT ONLY IS HE A TEAM ROPER AND STEER WRESTLER, HE IS ALSO AN EQUINE DENTIST AND FARRIER.

end of this cord is attached to the barrier mechanism, and the other end is looped over the calf's head just before the start. When the calf pulls on the mechanism, it releases the barrier rope in front of the rider's box and timing starts.

Every calf roper puts wraps and skid boots on his horse's legs, also making sure that the saddle, bridle, reins, and neck rope are properly fitted. He chooses his ropes according to the length of the arena and the weather conditions. He might apply more powder to his rope if the "feel" isn't just right: weather changes or humidity from an indoor arena can make a slight difference in the rope's feel and action. Looping one end of the lariat around his saddle horn, he holds onto the honda, shakes out the noose until it is about four or five feet, and evens up his coils. Then comes the wait—a space filled with stretching exercises, walking the horse, swinging the noose up and around to loosen it, re-coiling it again and again, and picturing the throw.

CASH MYERS AND HIS HORSE HAVE A GOOD START AFTER THIS CALF. CASH AND HIS BROTHER, ROPE, ARE PERENNIAL CONTENDERS FOR THE YEAR-END NATIONAL FINALS RODEO IN LAS VEGAS.

When the roper is called, a helper moves the calf to the front of the chute and stands behind it to make sure it faces straight ahead and is ready to go. The roper walks his horse into a box to the right of the calf and backs up into one corner, tucking the tail of his piggin' string in his back pocket or belt, and holding the loop in his mouth for easy access. He makes sure the coils and catch loop are just right, that the calf is set to go, and that his horse is standing squarely, paying attention. His nod is the signal to open the chute.

The Run

If the calves are fast and know where the exit is, the run, start to finish, might only take seven or eight seconds, with winners separated by hundredths of a second. The moment the chute man releases the gate, the calf heads into the arena, usually at a full run. As it reaches the predetermined scoreline and trips the rope barrier across the rider's chute, horse and rider can

legally start. Should the horse "break the barrier" rope first, the rider will receive a ten-second penalty and be out of the money before he has even had a chance to throw his rope. He'll continue with the run without knowing the judge's decision, because his timing is critical and his concentration can't be broken.

With lasso swinging, and horse and calf both approaching thirty mph, the cowboy makes one quick throw. Once the loop is in the air, the roper makes a decision. If he thinks he might have missed, he can, without penalty, get set to use his spare rope for another try. But if the

HAVING THROWN HIS LOOP, JEROME SCHNEEBERGER WILL TAKE UP THE SLACK AND BE READY TO
DISMOUNT, ALL IN A MATTER OF SECONDS

throw felt good, he'll pull back the reins, signaling his horse to put on the brakes. Whether on
the first or second try, the loop of his rope must go completely over the calf's head.

Although it's standard practice to mount and dismount a horse on its left side, calf ropers
dismount from the right to approach their calves. They've been doing this since the early

A GOOD EXAMPLE OF THE
DRAMATIC MOVEMENT A HORSE
CAN MAKE WHEN ASKED TO STOP
QUICKLY. THE STRAIGHT LINE OF
HIS BODY AS HE PUTS ON THE
BRAKES IS INDICATIVE OF THE
ATHLETICISM REQUIRED OF
TIMED-EVENT HORSES.

1960s, when two cowboys, Smith and Charter, discovered that, being right-handed (like most ropers), they could maintain constant contact with the rope they threw if they didn't have to first duck under their horses' necks. The result was a faster time. Smith and Charter used the technique to qualify for the National Finals Rodeo, and the method quickly spread. But this dismount can be tricky and has sent many a top rider to knee surgery. A roper has to have one foot on the ground at the same time his rope is settling around the calf and his horse is changing from full speed to a sliding halt.

The World Champion of 2001, Cody Ohl, credits his father, Leo, for getting him to where he is today. Cody grew up playing football and roping, but roping won out, and he has never looked back. "I've had a lot of ups and downs since my dad died. He was always around to motivate me, and it was pretty hard not to be able to call him anymore. He was the one who taught me to go out and win every time." Following a dip in his career and his spirit, Cody credits his recent successes to a change of attitude— and to his new horse, Hustler. Cody finished his championship year with a finale that will long be remembered. In the last round of the 2001 Wrangler National Finals Rodeo, he caught his calf, but only after it swerved to the side. He dismounted quickly in an attempt to make up time, and put too much torque on his knee in the process. Feeling the pain but wanting his final run to count, he crawled to the calf, made a correct tie to satisfy roping rules, and collapsed on the ground. Following knee surgery and many months of recuperation, Cody headed back toward the winner's circle.

The calf roper's goal is to reach a standing calf after dismounting. If the calf has fallen, rules state that he must first pick it up, high enough that the judge can see daylight between the calf and the ground, before he is allowed to flank it. While his horse is still in the process of stopping, the roper dismounts, controlling the tension on the rope so he can buffer the calf from being jerked abruptly. Not only does he want to reach a standing calf, he also risks being penalized if it gets flipped backwards. Then he runs toward his calf, maintaining contact with the rope by feeding it through his hand. Ideally, every roper wants to reach a calf that almost jumps into his hands, so all he has to do is lay it down. He will grab his rope close to the calf's neck for better leverage, pick it up, and flank it. As it goes down, he slides his left hand along the front leg, keeping contact with it while he gathers up the back feet—on a kicking calf, that's easier said than done. A good horse helps this critical process by backing up until it feels tension on the rope. That way, the calf will not feel any slack, so it's less likely to think it can struggle free. However, if a horse continues to back up enough to drag the calf along the

A CHAMPION SHOWS THE CORRECT WAY TO FLANK A CALF. IN THE BACKGROUND, CASH'S
HORSE WILL BACK UP UNTIL IT FEELS TENSION IN THE ROPE.

ground, not only will judges consider a penalty, but the cowboy will have a much harder time trying to make his tie.

Once the roper has gathered three legs together, he uses his piggin' string to make two or three wraps around the feet, finishing the tie with a "hooey," or half hitch. The method of tying and the number of wraps needed to secure a calf's legs can take milliseconds off a ticking clock. A roper who knows how crucial his timing is, for example, might decide to take a chance and save milliseconds by making only one wrap and a half hitch instead of two. He is gambling, in a sense, that a single wrap will be strong enough to hold the legs together. He also is well aware that the calf has a much better chance of kicking free. The moment he finishes, he throws both hands in the air, signaling the judge to drop the flag and stop the clock.

Before his time becomes official, the cowboy must return to his horse, remount, and walk a few steps forward to loosen the rope. Then, if the calf stays tied for six seconds, his time is recorded. If it kicks free before those long seconds pass, however, he'll get the score of "no time." Once the judge signals his decision, two helpers quickly move in to untie the calf, help it up, and direct it toward the exit.

Jerome Schneeberger not only qualified for his fourth NFR in 2001, he won the Prairie Circuit championship that year and was able to stay closer to home, which is in Oklahoma. "I just told a reporter how much I like to be near home. We've gone to over 100 rodeos this year and I just can't wait

THE COWBOY IS IN GOOD POSITION. HE HAS LOOPED HIS ROPE AROUND THE CALF'S FRONT LEG AND WILL HOLD IT IN PLACE WHILE HE BRINGS THE BACK LEGS UP TO IT FOR THE TIE.

to be home for a while." Jerome's traveling partner is the well-known champion Herbert Theriot, from Poplarville, Mississippi. He often rides Theriot's horse, Easy, who was voted AQHA calf roping horse of the year in 2001.

Horses

Quick starting, quick stopping Quarter Horses are prerequisites for roping. They have the ability and sense to do many jobs in a short period of time. Not only do they have to stay in one place until cued to run, but they must be able to read and react to the speed and direction of the calf, staying behind it (and off

2002 WORLD CHAMPION CODY OHL MAKES HIS TIE.

Todd Suhn's horse keeps the rope taut while he follows it to the calf. His left hand will move to the base of the loop where he can better control the calf as he gets ready to flank it. He holds his piggin' string in his teeth, looped and ready.

CODY OHL RETURNS QUICKLY TO HIS HORSE AFTER COMPLETING THE TASK. HE KNOWS THAT HIS HORSE SHOULDN'T WORK LONGER THAN NECESSARY AND THAT THE CALF NEEDS TO BE FREED AS SOON AS JUDGING PERMITS.

to one side) at just the right distance. A roping horse acts entirely on its own once the rope has been thrown and the rider pulls back on the reins. This horse is expected to dig its haunches into the ground, stop hard, and back up just enough to tighten the rope that connects the saddle to the calf.

Calves

The breed of calves used in PRCA rodeos must be native, Brahma, or a similar cross. They must wear numbered ear tags or brands, and have been already weaned from their mothers. Roping calves are required to weigh between 220 and 280 pounds, which is about three times their weight at birth. By this time, they have thicker hides and a flexible body that protects them while they are being roped and tied. Many rodeos in the United States, and all in Canada, have rules that reduce the amount of stress placed on calves when they are roped. If they flip over backwards when reaching the end of the rope, a judge can stop the run or assess a fine. Calves can only be thrown to the ground by being "flanked." Also, they cannot be dragged along the ground once they are tied. Calves are only roped about thirty times before they become too large for this event.

Judges

Two judges observe the run from different angles. The starter, or foul line judge, stands close to the barrier box. The tie judge or field judge watches from further down the arena where he can see the catch and the tie. Following PRCA rules and guidelines, both judges may assess penalties, either by adding time to the clock or by giving the rider a final score of "no time." If a rider's horse breaks the barrier, ten seconds will be added to the final time. If the roper fails to properly catch, flank, or tie his calf, or if the calf kicks free of the rope, he will receive a score of zero. Judges are also very aware of avoiding undue stress on a calf and will penalize a rider or fine him if they feel it is warranted.

A COWBOY MOVES HIS HORSE FORWARD TO SLACKEN THE ROPE AND TEST HIS TIE.

Barrel Racing

RIDING SOME OF THE FASTEST HORSES IN RODEO, the barrel racer's task is relatively simple: to race her horse in a cloverleaf pattern around three barrels faster than any of her competitors. With the potential of winning between $100,000 and $200,000 annually, competition among the top pro riders is fierce—and hundredths of a second separate the champions from those that go home empty-handed. Barrel racing is the only professional rodeo event specifically for women. The sport started in Texas in the early 1940s as a way to encourage wives and girl-friends of rodeo cowboys to participate. It has since become a multi-million-dollar crowd-pleaser, where only a few rules and a time clock determine the winner. Although there are many barrel racing organizations that share similar rules and regulations, this event, held in conjunction with PRCA-approved rodeos, is governed by the Women's Pro Rodeo Association (WPRA).

Barrel racing begins and ends at a dead run, with time starting when the horse's nose crosses a predetermined line. This line is marked with an electronic eye and backed up by a timer who watches for the judge to signal the beginning and end of a run. As with other timed events, the judge is responsible for determining penalties, which are assessed in seconds and added to the final time. Three 55-gallon steel barrels are set in a very specific triangular pattern approved by the WPRA. When called by the judge, a contestant enters the arena, heading toward her first barrel at full speed. She can choose to go left or right. If, for example, she guides her horse toward the right barrel, her first turn will be clockwise. The second and third barrels must then be negotiated counterclockwise, and vice versa. To make a clean run, she has to follow the required "clover-leaf" pattern without knocking over any barrels. Touching or moving a barrel is not a penalty, but five seconds are added to the final time for each barrel that tips over.

KRISTIE PETERSON, OF ELBERT, COLORADO, ON BOZO.

Winning runs vary from rodeo to rodeo, due to weather conditions or arena size, but a mere seventeen seconds is what the fans expect to see.

A professional barrel racer may enter an unlimited number of rodeos throughout the year, but she has definite travel time considerations and rarely more than one horse to compete on. She often travels alone or with a family that might consist of a couple of dogs, but she doesn't usually team up with fellow competitors. If she's successful, forty rodeos per year might earn a good living, a berth in the National Finals Rodeo in Las Vegas, or the WPRA Championships. But it can also take more than a hundred rodeos and one hundred thousand miles to be among the top-paid pros on the national circuit. Barrel racing can be a tough and sometimes very lonely life.

> *Four-time world champion Kristie Peterson didn't race barrels as a pro until after she was married and raising a family. A neighbor down the road was selling a, four-year-old sorrel stallion. She liked the looks of this horse and bought him for $400.00 Together, Kristie and Bozo have made history. She travels all over the United States and Canada with mechanic/husband, Chuck—and Bozo. When time permits, her daughter Jordan comes too. She organizes her rodeo schedule carefully now, after more than eight years of qualifying for the National Finals Rodeo, but she's still going strong. "There is the emotional side of travel and competition that no one realizes. All of the money and effort, the peaks and valleys. Sometimes it's just hard to keep up the momentum and attitude. But I love it and I owe everything to Bozo. The year coming up? It might be the best year yet."*

Barrel set-up

Before every rodeo begins, the first five barrel racers, not the judges or officials, are responsible for measuring and marking the spots where the barrels and the scoreline will be. An ideal arena for barrel racing is 300 by 150 feet. This provides adequate space for horse and rider to build speed before crossing the electronic scoreline and to turn around each barrel. The WPRA standard triangular pattern for such an arena calls for sixty feet from the electronic eye to the first barrel, ninety feet between the first and second barrel, and 105 feet between the second and farthest barrel. Barrel racers refer to this as the "seventeen-second pattern." Adjustments to this standard are made for larger or smaller arenas, which also means also that winning times will vary from the norm.

Training

Finding and training the right horse is a challenge. A barrel horse has to be built right, with good conformation and straight legs. He[1] must be fast and agile, with a natural ability to

---

1. Like most rodeo animals, horses in this event are of either gender. For the sake of simplicity and flow, it is easier to refer to a barrel horse as "he."

FULL OF TRY, THIS HORSE IS STRETCHED OUT IN A FINAL SPRINT TO THE FINISH. EVEN THOUGH HE KNOWS HIS JOB IS ALMOST DONE, HE DOES NOT ANTICIPATE WHERE THE STOP WILL BE UNTIL HIS RIDER PULLS UP ON THE REINS.

ALTHOUGH MOST RIDERS HAVE ONE EXCEPTIONAL BARREL HORSE, SHERRY CERVI HAS BEEN LUCKY ENOUGH TO FIND TWO IN HER CAREER: HAWK AND TROUBLES. THE 1995 AND 1999 WORLD CHAMPION DEMONSTRATES UNERRING BALANCE AS SHE MAKES HER FINAL TURN ON WELL-PLOWED GROUND.

change leads and use his body well. And he needs to have a sharp mind: willing to learn and able to perform under pressure. Above all, as champion Kristie Peterson says, "this type of horse has to have guts." A good trainer or rider can develop an animal with these qualities into a star performer—over time. It takes months for a barrel horse to learn when to run, when to slow down, and how to use his body when negotiating quick turns. It takes many more months for him to learn how to run and turn on all types of ground and under any conditions. During the entire training process, a barrel horse must develop a deep trust in his rider. Ultimately, it's the rider's judgment that he depends upon, because when training is done, he is going to try as hard as he can to do his job—even to the point of running through pain or injury.

A barrel horse is an exceptional athlete that must be kept in top mental and physical condition to withstand the pace of rodeo life—miles and miles of travel, new stalls, different water, and new grounds every few days. He stays motivated and in good shape by having excellent care and frequent workout changes. A barrel racer will mix up her horse's schedule by taking him on long trail rides, quiet workouts, or four-mile runs.

The barrel racer's own mental and physical condition is important as well. She has to find ways of dealing with the ups and downs of competitive life if she is to maintain a healthy sense of the sport and her place in it. Although this horsewoman might still be racing barrels at the age of fifty, she is the first to say that life on the road can be extremely demanding for the team of horse and rider.

Kristen Weaver has enjoyed many years in competition. She rides reining horses as well, and knows how much dedication and work is needed to turn pro. "There's a lot more to barrel racing than people realize. These horses have to be super athletes and mentally mature to perform week after week. Plus, you've got to take care of yourself. If both of us are in top physical and mental condition, well, that's what makes the difference between winning and losing."

Arrival and Preparation

A barrel racer makes sure her horse has adequate time to eat and rest before competing, often arriving at the rodeo grounds a day or two ahead of time. During this off-time, she makes her game plan, taking into account how her horse feels and what the arena and footing are like. If she feels her horse is tired or sore, she probably will not plan on pushing him. If the ground happens to be hard, which is often the case, she'll be thinking about how to help him during the turns and runs. Good judgment is the key here, because a top barrel horse is going to try his hardest, no matter what the conditions. The rider carries the responsibility of deciding whether to push or protect.

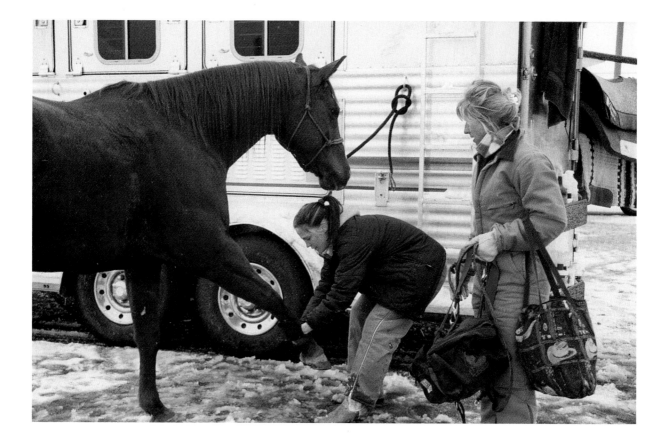

THREE-TIME NFR QUALIFIER WHO BROKE THE ARENA RECORD IN 2000, TONA WRIGHT TAKES A FEW MOMENTS TO STRETCH OUT MOE'S LEGS WHILE KELLY YATES HOLDS THE GEAR. THEY ARE APTLY DRESSED FOR SLACK ON A COLD IDAHO SPRING MORNING.

In the bigger rodeos, barrel racers have their first and sometimes second rounds of competition during early morning slack. They learn the order of their ride several days or weeks prior. The first five contestants drive stakes, with attached rope tails, deep into the ground to indicate barrel placement. They also mark the start line with a flag so the contractor or one of the officials can set up the wiring that goes to the electronic eye. Where the run begins is also agreed upon ahead of time. If the gate at the end of the arena is centered, then horses enter and exit at a run. If the gate is off to one side, the contestants must begin and end from within the arena itself.

An hour or two before competition, the riders will dress in the required manner: a long-sleeved shirt, colorful jeans, boots, and cowboy hat. They saddle up, walking or trotting wherever they can find space. Muscles must be stretched and loosened, necks and bodies flexed, minds mellowed to conserve energy. Every one of these horses knows what is in store. Finally, the horse's legs are protected with splint boots or polo wraps, and the hooves are covered by bell boots. Mental imaging and massage are additional ways a barrel racer prepares herself and her horse for competition. Often, a pair will be standing over to one side of the warm-up area, the rider's eyes closed, rehearsing the ride. Or she might have her hands cupped around her horse's front foot, pulling his leg gently forward and upwards to stretch the muscles. Or she may be sitting astride, using one rein to flex his long neck.

The Start

A big tractor methodically plowing the arena and making extra turns where the barrels will be placed is the signal that barrel racing is about to begin. Although footing is often not ideal, rodeo personnel recognize the need for a horse to run and turn in soft ground. An official usually oversees this process to make sure that the dirt has been adequately turned over—ridges on hard dirt can be just as tough on a horse's legs as wet or slippery ground. When the ground is loosened, helpers find the three short ropes that mark barrel placement. They bring in the barrels on the back of a pickup truck and place them over each rope. Another person, often someone working for the stock contractor, sets up the electronic eye that is now used in almost every pro rodeo. Racing commences when the judge nods for the first competitor to begin.

Every contestant knows the start order and where she is to begin. If the run begins from an alleyway that leads to the arena, she walks her horse around nearby, careful to avoid the prior contestant as she makes her exit. By this time, sights are set and any extra commotion goes unnoticed. When the official clears her to go, she moves her horse into position. As if taking aim at a target, both anticipate what to do next. Some of the horses need to be steadied by a helper while others will stay under control until they feel the reins loosen. Time begins when the horse explodes across the line marked with the electronic eye.

KRISTEN WEAVER TURNS AROUND THE MONEY BARREL, HER FIRST AND MOST CRITICAL TURN.

HAVING COMPLETED THE FIRST TURN, KRISTEN CHANGES HER FOCUS TO THE BARREL AHEAD.

Across the finish line at a full gallop.

The Run

In this event of horsemanship and timing, everything has to go just right during the entire run. Most critical is the judgment—of both horse and rider. A horse needs to try his hardest, whether racing forward or slowing to complete a turn, and the rider needs to know when to protect him and when to push hard. Crossing the start line at a gallop, she leans forward so her weight is over the horse's shoulder. They race toward the first barrel—left or right, depending upon how the horse has been trained. If the rider chooses the right barrel first, for example, the formula is automatic: right barrel, right turn, then two turns to the left, and head for home. Timing is critical when approaching a barrel. Any wrong move or signal can disrupt her horse's focus—just enough to move out of the money, or worse, cause an injury.

> Colorado's Kelly Yates knows about injury. She was second in the world standings at the end of 2001, but her horse strained its leg during a run in the Wrangler National Finals Rodeo and was out of commission for six months. Kelly's gray horse, Firewater Fiesta, has been an AQHA and Women's Pro Rodeo Association Horse of the Year.

The first barrel is often called the "money barrel" because it sets up the rest of the ride. Speed, excitement, lights, crowds, noise—everything is new when horse and rider make their entrance. And everything has to "click" during that first turn. With her eyes locked on the barrel, the cowgirl needs to sit down in the saddle at just the right moment, shifting her weight to cue the horse to slow down and prepare for the turn. Stabilizing her body with one hand on the horn, she feels for the right spot on her rein (sometimes marked with a knot) and uses it to tip the horse's nose inward toward the barrel. Although the horse has already changed leads in preparation for the turn, tipping his nose helps align him for the turn. Then she presses her inside leg and foot against her horse, helping him "shape" his body around the barrel. The barrel horse has to "rate" the barrel just like his rider, knowing how to adjust his speed to get around it without slipping. But his rider can either help or hinder during these dramatic turns—often negotiated at a 45-degree angle. She might inadvertently tip his nose to the outside because of where she was holding the rein, or shift her weight at just the wrong time, or push him too hard on ground he can't handle. Continuous adjustments help the pair around the "money barrel."

IN THIS PHOTO, GLORIA PUTS EQUAL WEIGHT IN BOTH STIRRUPS SO SHE CAN MOVE UP AND
FORWARD IN THE SADDLE, GIVING HER HORSE MORE FREEDOM TO SPRING AHEAD.

With the turn almost complete, the barrel horse gets his hooves into the ground and uses them as a platform to push forward, building momentum. When the ground is good, it allows him to show off his explosive skills. The second and third turns are made in the opposite direction of the first, but the same actions always apply: kick and hustle forward, cue to slow down and change leads, tip nose and press with the inside leg, then lean forward and go for broke. Should a barrel start to tip over, the rider can try to keep it standing by stabilizing it with her free hand. If the barrel falls over, she knows that the five-second penalty will put her out of the winnings, in which case she'll slow her horse a bit and save him from expending too much energy during the rest of his run. The horse can run flat out after circling the last barrel. Riders sometimes encourage this sprint with a crop or a few kicks, but a good barrel horse knows when it's time to run. No matter the result, a good ride is one that is fluid and efficient, with no slipping and no wasted motion.

Ruth Haislip appears to be taking a wider, more precautionary turn because of the ground. Though dry on the surface, it's still quite damp from a rainstorm on the previous day. A slip would not only hurt her time but also jeopardize her horse's legs.

GLORIA FREEMAN TAKES HER HORSE AROUND THE LAST BARREL, HELPING HIM THROUGH A TIGHT TURN. HIS FRONT LEGS ARE BRACED TO CONTINUE THE DIRECTION CHANGE, AND HE HAS PLANTED HIS BACK LEGS DEEP IN THE GROUND TO MAINTAIN BALANCE FOR THE REMAINDER OF THE TURN.

Ten-time world champion Charmayne James says that staying slim and in top physical condition helps her and her horse Scamper to succeed. But dieting and aerobics aren't the way she does it. While talking to the press, she told ProRodeo Sports News reporters: "When people ask me how I stay so thin, I tell them that I live on a ranch and that they would know if they followed me around."

Horses

Competitive barrel horses are fast and agile Quarter Horses, with good minds and a lot of "try." Although some have Thoroughbred in their bloodlines, they are not necessarily tall or high-strung. Regardless of size, a barrel horse must be built well enough to handle the pressure of

changing pace several times, connecting explosive sprints with three very tight turns. Often geldings—which have more even dispositions than mares or stallions—barrel horses reach their prime at age nine or ten and can remain competitive into their late teens. The search for a good barrel horse can be lengthy. Prices can vary greatly, ranging from a $500.00 feed lot horse to more than $50,000 for a solid winner. The best horses, even at double the price, will probably never come up for sale.

Judges

Although the clock is started and stopped with an electronic eye, there is always a judge in the arena and a time-keeper in the announcer's stand who records the time. The judge stands where he can see a horse's nose as it crosses the scoreline and the time-keeper watches for the judge to drop his flag—the signal that officially begins and ends each run. He will disqualify the rider if the cloverleaf pattern is not followed, and adds five seconds to the final time for every barrel knocked over.

KELLY YATES HEADS FOR THE TRAILER—AND ON TO ANOTHER RODEO IN THE SPRING OF 2002. YATES'S PRIMARY HORSE, FIESTA, WAS SIDELINED WITH A LEG INJURY SUSTAINED AT THE WRANGLER NATIONAL FINALS RODEO. KELLY IS A TOP COMPETITOR AND HAS ALREADY EARNED CLOSE TO HALF A MILLION DOLLARS IN HER CAREER.

KRISTIE PETERSON STANDS NEXT TO HER VERY SPECIAL HORSE, BOZO, DURING A BREAK AT THE 2002 DODGE NATIONAL CIRCUIT FINALS RODEO. BOTH ARE ATHLETES AS WELL AS COMPANIONS—A NECESSITY FOR THE WOMEN WHO CHOOSE TO ENTER THIS HIGHLY COMPETITIVE EVENT.

Ain't No Life After Rodeo

PAUL ZARZYSKI

There ain't no life after rodeo
Sulled-up old cowboys will tell you so

So when you feel your spur-lick weaken
And your bareback riggin' goes to leakin'

Bury your gripper elbow-deep
To hell with looking before you leap!

Fight those holts, sight down that mane
Spit in the face of age and pain

Give that hammerhead a hardware bath
Dazzle the judges with 90s math

Spur the rivets off your Wranglers
A capella rowels don't need *danglers*

Rake like a maniac, tick for tick
Tip your Resistol, flick the crowd's Bic

Fast-feet-fast-feet, gas-it-and-mash
Toes turned out with each jab and slash

Insanity, love, plus aggression
Call it passion, call it obsession

Adrenalined fury, 200 proof
Like guzzling moonshine up on the roof

Running on Bute, LeDoux songs and caffeine
You rollicking, rosined-up spurring machine

Too lazy to work, too scared to steal
Slaving for wages bushwhacks your zeal

So charge that front-end for those 8
You ain't no rodeo reprobate!

Grit each stroke out with every tooth
You're swimming the *cowboy* fountain of youth

Love that sunfish and love that high-dive
Believe you will ride 'til you're 95.

For Wayne Bronson, Tracy Mikes, Jerry Valdez,
Ted Kimzey, Bob Burkhart, Bill Larsen,
Del Nose, Deb Greenough . . .

From: *All this Way for the Short Ride* (Museum of New Mexico Press, 1996) by Paul Zarzyski.
Reprinted with the permission of the author.

Appendix: Statistics and Records

**W**ITH THE GROWING PRESTIGE OF THE PRCA, PBR, CRPA and WPRA, and their alliances with major sponsors and television networks, rodeo today is breaking records and generating interest like never before.

The season begins early in January, and for many cowboys, their first stop is the National Western Stock Show and Rodeo in Denver. It is one of the oldest and longest running rodeos in our country, drawing top contestants and an enthusiastic crowd. A big win early in the season helps pad the wallet and take some pressure off, but a cowboy must continue to stay within striking distance of his competitors during the rest of the year if he is to have a shot at the world championships. Midway through the year comes a chance to earn a lot of money during a short time: the Fourth of July series of rodeos that is referred to as "Cowboy Christmas." The official season ends 700 rodeos later, at the Cow Palace in San Francisco. Money won in this last big event might take a cowboy out of the running or boost him into the top fifteen in the world. If he makes the cut, he can compete in the highest paying rodeo of all: the National Finals Rodeo in Las Vegas.

Below are a few records and statistics of interest which are reprinted, with permission, from the PRCA's 2002 Media Guide. Other information can be easily accessed through Websites such as:

www.prorodeo.com (Professional Rodeo Cowboys Association)

www.pbrnow.com (Professional Bull Riders)

www.wpra.com (Women's Professional Rodeo Association)

www.rodeocanada.com (Canadian Professional Rodeo Association)

RAYNA PREWITT, SHOWS THE ATHLETICISM AND TIMING THAT ARE KEY TO A SUCCESSFUL TURN. HER HORSE IS DEEP IN THE DIRT, YET IT IS STILL BALANCED AND CONCENTRATING. RAYNA HAS HER LEG SET AGAINST HER HORSE AND A FIRM HAND ON THE REIN, WHICH WILL HELP SUPPORT AND GUIDE HIM THROUGH THE TURN. A BARREL RACER HAS TO KNOW HER HORSE'S ABILITIES AND DAY TO DAY CHANGES EXTREMELY WELL IN ORDER TO ASK FOR SUCH DRAMATIC MOVES.

The biggest PRCA rodeo sponsors in 2002, in alphabetical order:

Coors	Montana Silversmiths
Dodge	PRCA ProRodeo
Jack Daniel's	Resistol Hats
Justin Boots	U.S. Smokeless Tobacco Co.
Las Vegas Events	Wrangler

Highest-Paying PRCA Rodeos in 2001:

Las Vegas	$4,600,000
Cheyenne	$605,959
Dallas	$612,500
Houston	$559,690
Reno	$469,996
Denver	$441,798

THOUGH THEY MAY APPEAR RELAXED, MOST RODEO COWBOYS ARE EXTREMELY ORGANIZED AND FOCUSED WHEN PREPARING FOR COMPETITION. EACH HAS A PARTICULAR WAY OF CHECKING OVER EQUIPMENT, WRAPPING BOOTS AND GLOVES, PUTTING ON CHAPS AND VESTS. FOLLOWING A ROUTINE HELPS BLOCK OUT POSSIBLE DISTRACTIONS.

Professional Rodeo World Records

ALL-TIME PRCA CAREER EARNINGS LEADER
(Through 2001)

1. Joe Beaver (CR, TR, SR)	$2,071,160
2. Roy Cooper (CR, SR, TR, SW)	$2,056,548
3. Ty Murray (SB, BB, BR)	$1,913,623

HIGHEST EARNINGS IN A SINGLE SEASON
$297,896 by Ty Murray in 1993

MOST MONEY WON AT A RODEO
$124,821 by Ty Murray at 1993 NFR

MOST MONEY WON AT REGULAR-SEASON RODEO
$31,010 by Ty Murray at Houston Livestock Show and Rodeo in 1994

MOST MONEY WON IN ROOKIE YEAR
$107,806 by Matt Robertson (TR) in 2001

MOST MONEY WON IN ONE YEAR, BY EVENT
Bareback Riding: $185,556 by Lan LaJeunesse in 2001

Steer Wrestling: $176,584 by Rope Myers in 2001

Team Roping (Heading): $172,385 by Speed Williams in 1999

Team Roping (Heeling): $172,385 by Rich Skelton in 1999

Saddle Bronc Riding: $227,378 by Dan Mortenson in 1998

Calf Roping: $222,794 by Cody Ohl in 1998

Bull Riding: $174,772 by Blue Stone in 2001

Steer Roping: $99,132 by Guy Allen in 1998

MOST WORLD TITLES
Combination of events: 16, Jim Shoulders

All-Around: 7, Ty Murray

Consecutive All-Around: (tie) 6, Tom Ferguson, 1974-79 and Ty Murray, 1989-94

Bareback Riding: (tie) 5, Joe Alexander, Bruce Ford

Consecutive Bareback Riding: 5, Joe Alexander, 1971-75

Steer Wrestling: 6, Homer Pettigrew

Consecutive Steer Wrestling: 4, Homer Pettigrew, 1942-45

Team Roping: 7, Jake Barnes and Clay O'Brien Cooper

Consecutive Team Roping: 5, Jake Barnes and Clay O'Brien Cooper, 1985-89 and Speed Williams and Rich Skelton, 1997-2001

Saddle Bronc Riding: 6, Casey Tibbs

Consecutive Saddle Bronc Riding: 4, Casey Tibbs, 1951-54

Calf Roping: 8, Dean Oliver

Consecutive Calf Roping (tie): 5, Dean Oliver, 1960-64; Roy Cooper, 1980-84

Bull Riding: 8, Don Gay

Consecutive Bull Riding: 6, Jim Shoulders, 1954-59

Steer Roping: 16, Guy Allen

Consecutive Steer Roping: 11, Guy Allen, 1991-2001

YOUNGEST WORLD CHAMPION
Jim Rodriguez Jr., 1959 team roper at age 18

OLDEST WORLD CHAMPION
Ike Rude, 1953 steer roper at age 59

HIGHEST SCORED RIDES
Bareback Riding:
Joe Alexander, 93 points on Beutler Bros. & Cervi's "Marlboro" in Cheyenne, Wyo., 1974; Ty Murray, 92 points on Flying 5 Rodeo Co.'s "Bordertown" in San Francisco 1991

Saddle Bronc Riding:
Glen O'Neill, 95 points on Franklin's "Skoal's Airwolf" in Innisfail, Alberta, 1996; Doug Vold, 95 points on Franklin's "Transport" in Meadow Lake, Saskatchewan, 1979

Bull Riding:
Wade Leslie, 100 points on Growney's "Wolfman" in Central Point, Ore., 1991; Denny Flynn, 98 points on Steiner's "Red Lightning" in Palestine, Ill., 1979; Don Gay, 97 points on RSC's "Oscar" in San Francisco, 1977

FASTEST TIMES ON RECORD
(Arena conditions, sizes, and scorelines vary)

Steer Wrestling:
Oral Zumwalt, 2.2 seconds (without barrier) in the 1930s; (tie) Jim Bynum and Todd Whatley in Marietta, Okla., 1955, Gene Melton in Pecatonia, Ill., 1976, and Carl Deaton in Tulsa, Okla., 1976, 2.4 seconds (with barrier)

Team Roping:
Blaine Linaweaver and Jory Levy 3.5 seconds in San Angelo, Texas; Bob Harris and Tee Woolman, 3.7 seconds in Spanish Fork, Utah, 1986; (tie) Dee Pickett and Mike Beers, in Abilene, Texas, 1983, and Doyle Gellerman and Britt Bockius, Las Vegas (NFR), 1995, Speed Williams and Rich Skelton, Las Vegas (NFR), 1998, 3.8 seconds

Steer Roping:
Guy Allen, 8.1 seconds in Coffeyville, Kan., 1996

Calf Roping:
Lee Phillips, 5.7 seconds in Assiniboia, Saskatchewan, 1978 (did not leave box); Joe Beaver, 6.7 seconds in West Jordan, Utah, 1986; Cody Ohl, 6.8 seconds in Billings, Mont., 1995; Jeff Chapman, 6.8 seconds at NFR, 1997; Stran Smith, 6.8 seconds in Dallas, Texas (Summer Copenhagen Cup Finale), 2001; Cody Ohl, 6.8 seconds in Dallas, Texas (Summer Copenhagen Cup Finale), 2001

PRCA Annual Statistics, 1953-2001

Year	States with Rodeos	Number of Rodeos	Number. of Performances	Members	Permit Holders	Total Prize Money
2001	40*	688	2,015	5,913	2,544	$33,106,770
2000	39*	688	2,081	6,255	3,249	32,312,786
1999	42*	700	2,128	7,403	3,511	31,062,127
1998	42*	703	2,125	7,301	4,177	29,920,412
1997	44*	729	2,213	7,178	4,197	28,040,302
1996	46*	742	2,229	7,084	4,141	26,427,401
1995	43*	739	2,217	6,894	3,835	24,510,585
1994	46*	782	2,245	6,415	3,346	23,063,793
1993	43*	791	2,269	5,760	2,888	21,290,343
1992	41*	770	2,203	5,714	2,857	20,252,088
1991	41*	798	2,241	5,748	3,006	19,217,035
1990	42*	754	2,159	5,693	3,290	18,163,073
1989	40*	741	2,128	5,560	3,584	16,879,429
1988	41*	707	2,037	5,479	3,310	15,966,144
1987	41*	637	1,832	5,342	2,746	14,855,747
1986	41*	616	1,868	5,603	2,700	16,015,358
1985	41*	617	1,887	5,239	2,534	15,087,776
1984	39*	643	1,936	5,324	2,911	13,776,848
1983	42*	650	1,964	5,353	2,929	14,126,700
1982	42	643	1,936	5,461	4,105	13,187,610
1981	45	641	1,941	5,391	4,478	11,986,848
1980	43	631	1,921	5,114	4,038	9,936,760
1979	42	640	1,937	4,978	3,869	8,762,629
1978	39	618	1,890	4,820	4,364	8,085,309
1977	40	579	1,763	4,153	3,784	6,966,910
1976	36	586	1,974	4,027	4,025	6,690,100
1975	39	594	1,817	3,651	5,084	6,432,580
1974	40	590	1,816	3,583	4,304	5,386,884
1973	41	600	1,755	3,519	3,384	4,982,967
1972	42	567	1,691	3,144	2,707	4,375,110
1971	42	539	1,621	3,153	2,296	4,026,743
1970	42	547	1,653	3,446	2,821	4,155,021
1969	40	533	1,615	3,346	2,569	3,850,345
1968	41	521	1,592	3,159	2,379	3,685,629
1967	42	537	1,673	3,039	2,362	3,649,755
1966	44	524	1,602	3,007	2,344	3,452,544
1965	42	542	1,666	3,205	3,291	3,568,360
1964	44	591	1,795	3,105	3,361	3,665,469
1963	41	582	1,738	2,829	3,294	3,511,247
1962	37	540	1,587	2,670	2,837	3,080,102
1961	37	542	1,667	2,795	2,795	3,013,243
1960	35	509	1,583	2,820	3,709	3,086,920
1959	38	493	1,566	2,781	4,256	3,192,745
1958	35	475	1,535	2,809	3,131	2,792,107
1957	33	458	1,475	2,958	1,263	2,795,195
1956	33	519	1,699	3,329		2,862,525
1955	36	542	1,751	3,184		2,829,984
1954	34	550	1,721	3,284		2,726,190
1953	35	578	1,779	3,001		2,492,856

*AND 4 CANADIAN PROVINCES.

PRCA Stock of the Year

2001 SB Skoal's Painted Smile, Kesler Rodeo

BB Skoal's Cool Alley, Kesler Championship Rodeo

BULL Copenhagen Hurricane, Stace Smith Pro Rodeos

2000 SB (tie) Skoal's Spring Fling, Big Bend Rodeo Company and Surprise Party Skoal, Sankey Rodeo

BB Copenhagen Comotion, Beutler and Gaylord

BULL Skoal's Border Patrol, Flying Five Rodeo Company

1999 SB Skoal's Spring Fling, Big Bend Rodeo Company

BB Copenhagen Comotion, Beutler and Gaylord

BULL Skoal's Yellow Jacket, Flying Five Rodeo Company

1998 SB Skoal's Wild Card, Sankey Rodeo Company

BB Copenhagen Comotion, Beutler and Gaylord

BULL Skoal's King Kong, Rafter H Rodeo Livestock

1997 SB Skitso Skoal, Sankey Rodeo

BB Skoal's Spring Fling, Big Bend Rodeo Company

BULL Rapid Fire, Big Bend Rodeo Company

1996 SB Kingsway Skoal, Franklin Rodeo Stock

BB Khadafy Skoal, Powder River Rodeo Productions

BULL Dodge Ram Tough, Growney Brothers Rodeo

1995 SB Kingsway Skoal, Franklin Rodeo Stock

BB Khadafy Skoal, Powder River Rodeo Productions

BULL Bodacious, Andrews Rodeo Company

1994 SB Skitso Skoal, Sankey Rodeo Company

BB Lonesome Me Skoal, Calgary Stampede

BULL Bodacious, Andrews Rodeo Company

1993 SB Bobby Joe Skoal, Harry Vold Rodeo Company

BB Skoals Airwolf, Franklin Rodeo Stock

BULL Grasshopper, Western Rodeos Inc.

1992 SB Bobby Joe Skoal, Harry Vold Rodeo Company

BB High Chaparral Copenhagen, Bar T Rodeo Company

BULL Copenhagen Rocy, Western Rodeos

1991 SB Bobby Joe Skoal, Harry Vold Rodeo Company

BB Satan's Skoal, Dorenkamp

BULL Skoal's Outlaw Willie, Andrews Rodeo Company

1990 SB Lonesome Me Skoal, Calgary Stampede

BB Khadafy Skoal, Powder River Rodeo Productions

BULL Skoal's Pacific Bell, Western Rodeos

1989 SB Lonesome Me Skoal, Calgary Stampede

BB High Chaparral Copenhagen, Don Peterson

BULL Skoal's Pacific Bell, Western Rodeos

1988 SB Skoal's Alley Cat, G. Kesler

BB Kingsway Skoal, Franklin Rodeo Stock

BULL Skoal's Pacific Bell, Western Rodeos

1987 SB (tie) Challenger & Skoal, Beutler & Son and Kloud Grey Skoal, Calgary Stampede

BB Skoal's Sippin' Velvet, Bernis Johnson

BULL Red Rock, Growney Bros.

1986 SB Wrangler Savvy, Harry Vold Rodeo Company

BB Sippin' Velvet, Bernis Johnson

BULL Mr. T, Burns Rodeo Company

1985 SB Blow Out, Beutler & Son

BB Tombstone, Jim Sutton

BULL Cowtown, Beutler & Son

1984 SB Try Me, Wayne Vold

BB (tie) Sippin' Velvet, Bernis Johnson and Lonesome Me, Calgary Stampede

BULL No. 105, Dell Hall

1983 SB Alibi, Dell Hall

BB Sippin' Velvet, Bernis Johnson

BULL Oscar's Velvet, Christensen Bros.

1982 SB Buckskin Velvet, Flying U

BB Smith & Velvet, Bobby Christensen

BULL Savage 7, Steiner

1981 SB Rusty, Harry Vold Rodeo Co.

BB Classic Velvet, Flying U

BULL (tie) Savage 7, Steiner and No. 105, Dell Hall

1980 SB Brookman's Velvet, Cervi Championship

BB Smith & Velvet, Christensen Bros.

JOE BEAVER RETURNS TO HIS PALOMINO THAT IS STANDING STILL, BUT ANCHORED IN WAIT. EYES AND EARS ARE AWAITING DIRECTION FROM THE RIDER—A PERFECT DEMONSTRATION BY THIS PARTNER IN ROPING.

	BULL	No. 777, Harry Vold Rodeo Co.
1979	SB	(tie) Angel Sings, Harry Vold Rodeo Co. and Deep Water, Jim Sutton
	BB	Smith & Velvet (formerly Mr. Smith), Christensen Bros.
	BULL	No. 777, Harry Vold Rodeo Co.
1978	SB	Angel Sings, Harry Vold Rodeo Co.
	BB	Sippin' Velvet, Bernis Johnson
	BULL	#11, Red Lightning, Steiner
1977	SB	Crystal Springs, Bob Barnes
	BB	Mr. Smith, Christensen Bros.
	BULL	General Isomo, Beutler Brothers and Cervi
1976	SB	Sarcee Sorrel, Harry & Wayne Vold

	BB	Moon Rocket, Calgary Stampede
	BULL	Panda Bear, Harry Vold Rodeo Co.
1975	SB	Frontier Airlines, Beutler Brothers and Cervi
	BB	Stormy Weather, Steiner
	BULL	(tie) Tiger, Cervi Rodeo Co. and Black 6, Tommy Steiner
1974	SB	Checkmate, Bobby Christensen
	BB	Smokey, Harry Vold Rodeo Co.
	BULL	Tiger, Billy Minick

FROM 1956–1973, ONLY ONE TOP BUCKING HORSE WAS NAMED EACH YEAR.

1973	Sam Bass, Jiggs Beutler
1972	Descent, Beutler Brothers & Cervi
1971	Descent, Beutler Brothers & Cervi

1970	Rodeo News, Reg Kesler
1969	Descent, Beutler Brothers & Cervi
1968	Descent, Beutler Brothers & Cervi
1967	Descent, Beutler Brothers & Cervi
1966	Descent, Beutler Brothers & Cervi
1965	Jake, Harry Knight
1964	Wanda Dee, Calgary Stampede
1963	Big John, Harry Knight
1962	Big John, Harry Knight
1961	Jesse James, Hoss Inman
1960	Jake, Harry Knight
1959	Trails End, Zumwalt Rodeo Co.
1958	(tie) Warpaint, Christensen Bros. and Joker, Harry Knight
1957	Warpaint, Christensen Bros.
1956	Warpaint, Christensen Bros.

2001 AQHA Horses of the Year

STEER WRESTLING

1. Bad Motor Scooter (Scooter); owner, Jimmy Powers; rider, Steve Duhon
2. (tie) Oh Lucky Guy (Doc); owner, Rod Lyman; riders, Rod Lyman, Frank Thompson
   The Stitch (Stitch); owners, Randy Suhn and Tim Segelke; riders, same

TEAM ROPING-HEADER

1. Smoothly Anchored (Calhoun); owner, Richard Eiguren; rider, same
2. Oklahoma Top Hat (Scooter); owner, Charles Pogue; rider, same

3. Precious Speck; owner, Travis Tryan; riders, Travis and Clay Tryan

TEAM ROPING-HEELER

1. Boons Smooth Val (Roany); owner, Rich Skelton; rider, same
2. Rafter L Bonnie Lad (Miami); owner, Dugan Kelly; rider, same
3. Seniors Podking (Senior); owner, Britt Bockius; rider, same

CALF ROPING

1. Leos Sen Bar (Easy); owner, Herbert Theriot; rider, same

2. Kid Taurus (Grumpy); owner, Brent Lewis; rider, same
3. Topofthemarket (Topper); owner, Trent Walls; rider, same

BARREL RACING

1. Firewater Fiesta (Fiesta); owner, Kelly Yates; rider, same
2. Jet Royal Speed (Hawk); owner, Sherry Cervi; rider, same
3. Zanzaco (Moe); owner, Lonnie and Patty Wright; rider, Tona Wright

Rodeo Associations

American Indian Rodeo Association of Oklahoma (AIRAO)
Alabama High School Rodeo Association
Alaska Barrel Racers Association
American Calf Ropers Association
American Junior Bull Riders Association
American Junior Rodeo Association
American Professional Rodeo Association

American Professional Rodeo Clowns and Bullfighters Association
American Quarter Horse Association
Arkansas Roughstock Association
Australian Professional Rodeo Association
Barrel Futurities of America
B.C. Rodeo
B.C., Surrey

B.C., Williams Lake
British Columbia Team Penning Assoc.
California Pro Rodeo Circuit
Canadian Intercollegiate Rodeo Association
Canadian Professional Rodeo Association
CWHR (Canada)
Cheyenne Frontier Days
Colorado High School Rodeo Association

TIM PARKER, A BUSINESSMAN AND FARRIER FROM WENDELL, IDAHO, WARMS UP THREE BULLDOGGING HORSES. TIM'S FIRST PRIORITY IS TO HAZE FOR HIS SON, T.J. THE TWO SPEND A GOOD DEAL OF TIME ON THE ROAD, WITH EXCELLENT HORSES AND MANY WINS.

Colorado Pro Rodeo Association
Cowboy Heritage Association of America
CPRA (Cowboys Pro Rodeo Association)
Cypress Fairbanks Rodeo Association
East Texas Barrel Racing Association
Friends of Rodeo
GPIRA (Great Plains Indian Rodeo Association)
INFR (Indian National Finals Rodeo)
IPRA (International Professional Rodeo Association)
International Team Penning Association
Iowa Rodeo Cowboys Association
Lone Star High School Rodeo Association
Maine Barrel Racing Association Homepage
MidStates Rodeo Association
Minnesota Rodeo Association
Missouri Rodeo Cowboy Association
Montana Team Ropers Association
NBRA (National Barrel Racing Association)

National Barrel Horse Association
National Cowboy Hall of Fame
National Cowgirl Hall of Fame
National High School Rodeo Association
National Intercollegiate Rodeo Association
National Little Britches Rodeo Association
National Pro Rodeo Association
National Rodeo Council of Australia
NZRCA (New Zealand Rodeo Cowboy Association)
North American Bull Riding Association
North Dakota Rodeo Association
NPRFA (Northwest Pro Rodeo Association)
Okinawa Bull Riding Association
Ontario Rodeo Association
Prairie Indian Rodeo Association
Professional Armed Forces Rodeo Association
PBR (Professional Bull Riders)
Professional Women's Rodeo Association
PRCA (Professional Rodeo Cowboys Association)

Pro Rodeo Canada
Pro-West Rodeo Association
Pueblo West Rodeo Association
RMIRA (Rocky Mountain Indian Rodeo Association)
RMRA (Rocky Mountain Rodeo Association)
Rodeo B.C.
Senior Pro Rodeo (National Old Timers Rodeo Association)
South Dakota Rodeo Association
Southeast Texas Team Penners Association
Southern Pro Bull Riders Association
Southern Rodeo Association
Texas Cowboys Rodeo Association
U.S. Calf Ropers Association
United Rodeo Association
United States Team Roping Championships
Women's Professional Rodeo Association
Working Ranch Cowboys Association